AUTISM SPECTRUM DISORDER AND THE
TRANSITION INTO SECONDARY SCHOOL

of related interest

**Successful School Change and Transition
for the Child with Asperger Syndrome**
A Guide for Parents
Clare Lawrence
ISBN 978 1 84905 052 4
eISBN 978 0 85700 358 4

Making the Move
A Guide for Schools and Parents on the Transfer
of Pupils with Autism Spectrum Disorders (ASDs)
from Primary to Secondary School
K.I. Al-Ghani and Lynda Kenward
Illustrated by Haitham Al-Ghani
ISBN 978 1 84310 934 1
eISBN 978 1 84642 935 4

**Achieving Successful Transitions
for Young People with Disabilities**
A Practical Guide
Jill Hughes and Natalie Lackenby
ISBN 978 1 84905 568 0
eISBN 978 1 78450 005 4

**Helping Children with Autism Spectrum Conditions
through Everyday Transitions**
Small Changes – Big Challenges
John Smith, Jane Donlan and Bob Smith
ISBN 978 1 84905 275 7
eISBN 978 0 85700 572 4

AUTISM SPECTRUM DISORDER AND THE **TRANSITION INTO SECONDARY SCHOOL**

A Handbook for Implementing Strategies in the Mainstream School Setting

Marianna Murin, Josselyn Hellriegel and Will Mandy

With contributions from:

Professor David Skuse, Chair of Behavioural and Brain Sciences, Institute of Child Health and Lead of the National Centre for High Functioning Autism, Great Ormond Street Hospital for Children

Sara M. Staunton, Senior Speech and Language Therapist, Linn Dara Child and Adolescent Mental Health Service

Seonaid Anderson, Research Psychologist, Institute of Child Health

Dr Liz Searle, Consultant Child and Adolescent Psychiatrist, Tavistock and Portman NHS Trust

Lucy Watson, Assistant Psychologist, National Centre for High Functioning Autism, Great Ormond Street Hospital for Children

Jack K. Nejand, Undergraduate Psychology Student on Placement, National Centre for High Functioning Autism, Great Ormond Street Hospital

Jessica Kingsley *Publishers*
London and Philadelphia

First published in 2016
by Jessica Kingsley Publishers
73 Collier Street
London N1 9BE, UK
and
400 Market Street, Suite 400
Philadelphia, PA 19106, USA

www.jkp.com

Library of Congress Cataloging in Publication Data
A CIP catalog record for this book is available from the Library of Congress

British Library Cataloguing in Publication Data
A CIP catalogue record for this book is available from the British Library

ISBN 978 1 78592 018 9
eISBN 978 1 78450 262 1

Printed and bound in the United States

CONTENTS

ACKNOWLEDGEMENTS

We would first like to thank the children, parents, schools and other professionals who gave so generously of their time in completing questionnaires, tests, interviews and focus groups as part of the Supporting Children in Education (Transitions) Study. We are grateful also to those from across the UK and Ireland, whom we will never have the opportunity to meet, but who kindly took the time to complete our online questionnaire for the study.

We would especially like to thank our Transitions research team – Seonaid Anderson, research psychologist, and Sara Staunton, senior speech and language therapist. This manual is based on the three-year research study at the Behaviour and Brain Sciences Unit at the Institute of Child Health led by Seonaid and Sara. It is due to their hard work and passion for supporting children with ASD in education that we were able to evaluate how effective this intervention is and whether it makes a real difference in facilitating a successful transition.

This manual could not have been completed without the support, mentorship and enthusiasm of Professor David Skuse, the Head of the Behaviour and Brain Sciences Unit, who was the Principal Investigator on the project and enabled the study to happen. An internationally renowned expert in the field of ASD, his high ambition for children with ASD, his tireless curiosity about new perspectives and his remarkable energy will be source of inspiration always. In all these years of working together, David has been the most positive person to work with. We very much hope this approach has translated through his supervision to the manual and the intervention outlined.

Our special acknowledgements go to colleagues who contributed significantly to this book. Sara Staunton, Senior Speech and Language Therapist in the team, for her invaluable expertise on communication difficulties children with ASD tend to experience. Sara wrote the chapter on Language Difficulties and helped to complete the manuscript with her amazing editing skills. Seonaid Anderson, our Research Psychologist, for contributing with the 'Sensory Sensitivities' chapter and Dr Liz Searle, Consultant Child and Adolescent Psychiatrist, for her expertise and work on the chapter on 'Conditions that Co-Occur with ASD'. We would like to extend our special thanks to two more contributors to this book: Lucy Watson, for co-authoring 'My Transition Workbook' section, and Jack Nejand, for his very creative approach to writing the section on Relaxation Strategies. Their valuable contributions enabled this intervention to benefit from multidisciplinary approach, which is so essential for children with ASD.

Thank you to the placement students, volunteers and staff at the Institute of Child Health and Great Ormond Street Hospital who helped us in many different capacities during the Transitions Study, in particular: Ozlem Baykaner, Hannah Tobin, Royston Hall, Catherine Walters, Catherine Walkin, Harriet Boyd, Rachel Taylor, Nicola Coop, Claudia Willis, Abigail Carter, Sonya Tsancheva,

Dr Louise Slator, Rosie Kemp, Dr Rebecca Varrall, Sameera Ahmed, Goh Mei Fang, Fiona Roberts, Sophie Bellringer, Dr Sarah Brown, Conchi Vera-Valderrama, Natalia Katting, Eleonore Bristow, Kate Wilcocks and Britt Pederson.

Thank you to the professionals from the fields of education and psychology who gave generously of their time in advising us regarding the content of the Transition Pack and/or the design of the Study: Liesel Batterham, Helen Bull, Kate Ripley, Pat Markwardt, Jo Brooks, Dr Bettina Hohnen, Dr Stephanie King, Nicola Lowe, the special rducational needs coordinators from Kingston LEA, Prof. Tony Charman and Dr Liz Pellicano.

We would like to extend warm particular thanks to the following people for all their help, support and advice regarding the creation of this pack: Dr Naomi Dale, Head of Psychology (Neurodisability), The Wolfson Neurodisability Service, Great Ormond Street Hospital, London; Professor Norah Frederickson, Director, Educational Psychology Group Department of Clinical, Educational and Health Psychology, University College London; Alice Stobart, formerly of National Autistic Society National Autistic Society; Caroline Hattersley, Head of Information, Advice and Advocacy, National Autistic Society.

On a personal level, I would like to thank Kerry Barner. Fabulous writer, editor and loyal friend that she is, only she will know how many informal lessons in English it took to enable me to write this…

Finally, we would like to extend our thanks to the Great Ormond Street Hospital Children's Charity and its supporters, for enabling us to conduct the Supporting Children in Education (Transitions) Study under which this pack was created and evaluated. Donations to the GOSH Children's Charity can be made at www.gosh.org.

INTRODUCTION AND INSTRUCTIONS FOR THE TRANSITION PACK

 ## HOW WAS THE IDEA BORN?

At the Social Communication Disorders Clinic (SCDC) at Great Ormond Street Hospital (GOSH) we are often asked how best to support children with autism spectrum disorder (ASD) through their transition from primary to secondary school. There are lots of examples of good practice from special educational needs coordinators (SENCOs), teachers and autism support teams. As there are no clear national guidelines for transition support, most packages that have been developed are created by committed individuals in their schools or local areas. We have been very fortunate to work with a wide range of highly dedicated school professionals and parents/carers who have contributed their ideas, resources and time to the creation of this resource pack which aims to help children with ASD. This pack has been produced as part of a research project during which we are hoping to measure the outcomes of well-planned transitions.

 ## WHY IS TRANSITION MORE CHALLENGING FOR PUPILS WITH ASD?

Transition from primary to secondary school can be a daunting and anxiety-provoking move for all pupils, as well as their parents/carers. Pupils with ASD can be particularly vulnerable during this period, as they can often find even minor changes challenging. Their vulnerability is exacerbated by their difficulties with expressing their anxiety or asking for help. Children with ASD may have difficulties with predicting and adapting to new situations. This, as well as their difficulties in flexible thinking, can provoke anxiety. Social situations with 'unwritten rules' can be particularly challenging for pupils with ASD. The novelty and complexity of social situations in secondary school can lead to isolation and low self-esteem. Furthermore, pupils with ASD often tend to have a number of 'invisible' disabilities, such as sensory sensitivities, which can make seemingly simple tasks, such as eating lunch in a busy canteen, extremely difficult.

Although a child may appear to be coping well initially, it is important to be aware that accumulated frustration can often lead to significant problems, such as behavioural difficulties, school avoidance, social isolation or academic underachievement, which may become apparent only after a while. *A proactive stance towards this can be invaluable, with long-term benefits for the whole of the child's school career.*

WHAT IS STEP-ASD?

The Systemic Transition in Education Programme for ASD (STEP-ASD) has been designed to cover the *full range* of the most frequent support needs of pupils on the autism spectrum. Children have their own specific profile of strengths and support needs and this pack will be individualised for a particular child making the transition. This pack has been designed to be *individualised* for each pupil, therefore teachers are NOT expected to use the entire pack but to use the relevant sections. For example, sensory sensitivities may be important for one child, but other pupils with ASD may not have any difficulties in this area at all. This means that only certain chapters of the pack will be relevant for a particular child.

WHAT IS THE EVIDENCE FOR STEP-ASD?

With any intervention, it is important to ask 'does it work?' and 'can it be implemented in the real world?' We have conducted a research project to address these questions. Our strategy was to follow a group of children with ASD making the transition from primary to secondary school, and to see how they managed in terms of their emotional and behavioural functioning. In phase one of the project we simply observed the school transition, without giving STEP-ASD. We wanted to learn what sorts of difficulties children with ASD faced when they moved from primary to secondary education receiving no additional support from us. We used some of the things we learnt in phase one to design STEP-ASD. Once we had done this, we moved to phase two of the project, in which we gave STEP-ASD to a new group of children with ASD, to see if it made a difference to their emotional and behavioural outcomes when they transitioned. We were interested to see if the children who had STEP-ASD had a better school transition than those who did not. We also interviewed teachers and other educationalists who had helped implement STEP-ASD about their experiences, to discover if they found it manageable and helpful.

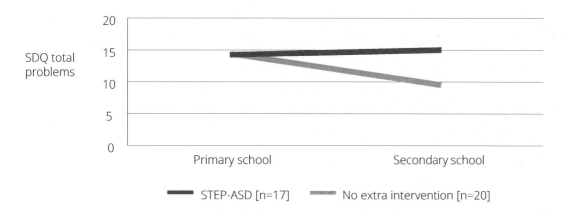

Figure I.1: Emotional, behavioural and social problems across school transition

This graph shows the difference between children with ASD who did and did not have STEP-ASD on the school-report version of the Strengths and Difficulties Questionnaire 'total problems' scale. This measures a range of emotional, behavioural and social difficulties that children can experience at school, with scores above 11 indicative of problems needing attention. As can be seen from the graph, the children who did not get STEP-ASD had high levels of total problems at the end of primary school, and these persisted into secondary school. By contrast, children who had STEP-ASD showed a large reduction in their total problems score over the transition. The two groups were very similar in many respects (age, intelligence, gender, severity of ASD, ethnicity, levels of received support), so it is unlikely that the different trajectories shown in the graphs arose because the STEP-ASD children had milder difficulties or more support outside of STEP-ASD. The most likely explanation is that STEP-ASD influenced the decline in their emotional, behavioural and social problems during school transition.

When we asked 15 educationalists (e.g. teachers, teaching assistants, head teachers) who had implemented STEP-ASD in schools, they were overwhelmingly positive about the intervention. For example, 14 (93%) said that they found the Transition Pack helpful and user-friendly. Twelve thought that STEP-ASD had improved their knowledge of ASD, and 14 (93%) said that they would recommend it to a colleague who needed to help a child with ASD make the school transition.

Our findings will need to be further tested in bigger and even more carefully conducted studies. However, initial evidence is promising, suggesting that school staff who implement STEP-ASD find it manageable and useful, and that STEP-ASD helps to reduce the emotional, behavioural and social difficulties during school transition.

If you would like to read more about the evidence for STEP-ASD you can find two papers we have written on our research in the journal *Autism*, which are freely available even if you do not have a subscription to the journal (Mandy *et al.*, 2015a, 2015b).

- Mandy, W., Murin, M., Baykaner, O., Staunton, S., Hellriegel, J., Anderson, S., & Skuse, D. (2015). The transition from primary to secondary school in mainstream education for children with autism spectrum disorder. *Autism*, doi 1362361314562616.

- Mandy, W., Murin, M., Baykaner, O., Staunton, S., Cobb, R., Hellriegel, J., Anderson, S., & Skuse, D. (2015). Easing the transition to secondary education for children with autism spectrum disorder – an evaluation of the Systemic Transition in Education Programme for ASD (STEP-ASD). *Autism*, doi 1362361314562616.

HOW IS IT TO BE USED?

STEP-ASD consists of three parts:

Part 1: Creating Individualised Transition Plan: The first chapter describes how to create an Individualised Transition Plan using Screening Questionnaires (Appendix 1 and 2) and organising a 'Bridge Meeting' conducted between the allocated professionals from the primary and secondary schools and the parents.	**Part 2: Management strategies:** The remaining chapters provide an overview of successful strategies used in the classroom for children with an ASD both in general (Chapter 1) and in relation to their specific needs, e.g. sensory sensitivities (Chapters 2–10).	**Part 3: Useful resources:** Finally the appendices provide examples and templates of all of the resources described throughout this package.

As a first step, the strengths and specific support needs of the child would be identified via Screening Questionnaires, which are completed by the child, their parents or carers and the allocated professional from the primary school. As a second step, the identified areas of the child's support needs are discussed at a 'Bridge Meeting' in the spring term when STEP-ASD would be presented and individualised for the particular child. The 'Bridge Meeting' is set up specifically to enable sharing of information between the primary and secondary schools, as well as the child and their parents. During the Bridge Meeting, an Individualised Transition Plan is created and relevant tasks from the STEP-ASD are divided between parents/carers and allocated staff members from the primary and secondary schools (please see Figure P.1 in the next section for a detailed outline of the important prerequisites and steps in creating a transition plan).

WHO IS IT FOR?

The Transition Pack can be implemented by secondary schools (teachers, SENCOs, TAs or LSAs) but it also aims to be a useful resource for primary school teachers, parents/carers and children which can be photocopied and distributed as needed.

PART ONE

CREATING AN INDIVIDUALISED TRANSITION PLAN

WHAT ARE THE BENEFITS OF A WELL-PLANNED TRANSITION?

There are general strategies that are helpful when planning a transition (Chapter 1). However, due to the significant variability of strengths and difficulties in children with ASD there are additional strategies which are provided by the resource chapters in this pack.

Investing time in preparing a pupil with ASD for this significant transition brings multiple benefits. It not only helps to reduce a pupil's severe anxiety but also prevents many secondary consequences such as struggling to cope academically, negative experiences and failure. It enables the pupil to cope with this challenge to the best of their ability. Not all pupils with ASD require support with all the strategies below, as each child will have their own individual strengths and difficulties. The strategies are intended to provide a helpful checklist of the most important areas on which to focus. This aims to give the pupil an equal chance of coping with this transition as successfully as their non-disabled peers. Whilst it is recognised that schools often do not have a sufficient level of resources to support children with ASD, it is hoped that the individual dedication of school professionals will reduce the difficulties these children experience in secondary school.

 HOW DO YOU CREATE AN INDIVIDUALISED TRANSITION PLAN?

The most important aspect of creating a support plan for a pupil with ASD is tailoring the support to the individual child's strengths and difficulties. What follows is an outline of important prerequisites and steps to create a transition plan.

Essential prerequisites	Creating an Individualised Transition Plan
Collaborative work	Step 1: Screening Questionnaires
Advance planning	Step 2: Bridge Meeting
Understanding ASD	Step 3: Transition Plan
	Step 4: Pupil Profile

Figure P.1: Prerequisites and steps in creating a transition plan

 ESSENTIAL PREREQUISITES

Collaborative work

ASD is so variable that it is essential to create a clear description of a child's difficulties and strengths. This information should be shared amongst the following:

- Allocated professional from the secondary school (teachers, SENCOs, TAs or LSAs)

- Allocated professional from the primary school (teachers, SENCOs, TAs or LSAs)

- Parents/carers of the pupil

- The pupil.

Information from any professional reports that may be important to consider, such as reports from educational or clinical psychologists, or speech and language therapists, should also be included.

Collaborative work is equally important because children with ASD frequently have difficulties with:

- **Generalisation:** For example, children may learn a new skill at school, but may not be able to transfer it into different environments, such as their home or community.

- **Different presentation in different environments:** For example, children with ASD may only be able to express their frustration in a highly familiar environment in which they feel 'safe', most often at home.

Advance planning

A transition plan may take six months to prepare because information needs to be gathered, evaluated and implemented by the primary and secondary schools, as well as the families. Also, children may need time to learn new skills essential to coping in a secondary school setting. Ideally, the creation of the Individualised Transition Plan should start in the spring term of Year 6.

Understanding ASD

WHAT IS AUTISM SPECTRUM DISORDER?

Autism spectrum disorder (ASD) is defined as a complex neurodevelopmental disability, which affects the way a person thinks and perceives the world around them, and how they interact with their environment. ASD is characterised by the following 'dyad of impairments':

- Difficulties with social relationships and social communication

- Difficulties with flexibility and sensory processing.

 ARE THERE DIFFERENT TYPES OF AUTISM SPECTRUM DISORDER?

Until recently, experts believed that there were different subtypes of ASD, which were sufficiently distinct from each other to need their own names. These were called:

- Autism (including high-functioning autism)

- Asperger's syndrome

- Atypical autism

- Pervasive developmental disorder – not otherwise specified.

However, it has become evident that there are no clear distinctions between these proposed subtypes of ASD, and even very experienced clinicians show little agreement on which subtype an individual has. As a result, the subtyping approach to ASD was recently abolished. These days the term ASD is used as an umbrella term for all different autistic presentations. Nevertheless, it is important to recognise that there is tremendous variability in the way that ASD affects people, and this needs to be reflected in the ways we understand and help those who have this diagnosis.

PREVALENCE OF ASD

Recent studies indicate that ASD affects approximately 1% of the population, and boys are more commonly diagnosed than girls. It can be more difficult to diagnose girls because they can often learn superficial social skills. The current prevalence ratios of somewhere between 1:3 and 1:4 diagnosed girls versus boys may therefore be an underestimate. Children who may not reach the threshold for a formal diagnosis, but who may display some of the symptoms, may also benefit from this handbook.

ADDITIONAL DIFFICULTIES

Research indicates that children with ASD are at significantly increased risk of having additional developmental problems, such as ADHD, or mental health and emotional difficulties, such as anxiety, depression or conduct problems (commonly known as comorbid conditions). There is still a debate about the exact prevalence rates of comorbid difficulties. However, all studies are consistent in reporting that 70–87% of children with ASD additionally meet criteria for at least one of the following diagnoses:

- ADHD

- Anxiety disorders (such as generalised anxiety disorder, obsessive-compulsive disorder or social phobia)

- Depression

- Conduct problems

- Dyspraxia

- Specific learning difficulties such as dyslexia or dyscalculia

- Executive function problems

- Tourette syndrome

- Feeding and eating disorders.

Please see Chapter 10 for further information: Conditions that Co-Occur with ASD.

CREATING AN INDIVIDUALISED TRANSITION PLAN

Creating an Individualised Transition Plan for the pupil will require the following steps:

Step 1: Screening Questionnaires

Step 2: Bridge Meeting

Step 3: Transition Plan

Step 4: Pupil Profile

Step 1: Screening Questionnaires

WHAT ARE SCREENING QUESTIONNAIRES?

In order to ensure individualised support tailored to the child's needs, Screening Questionnaires have been designed to identify areas of a pupil's strengths and support needs on a scale of priority. The initial section of each Screening Questionnaire focuses on obtaining general information about the child. The remaining sections are focused on the wide range of specific difficulties associated with ASD. However, as only certain areas will be relevant for each pupil, different (numbers, 1, 2 and 3) will signify the level of importance, so that attention can be focused on the key areas of each pupil's support needs. Only the identified priority areas will feed into the pupil's Transition Management Plan. Finally, the Screening Questionnaires have been designed in such a way that each section corresponds to a specific chapter of Part 2 of this handbook (in which the management strategies are outlined). As a result, once the priority areas have been identified by the Screening Questionnaires only the corresponding chapters of this pack will need to be used for the particular pupil.

WHO SHOULD COMPLETE SCREENING QUESTIONNAIRES?

There are two versions of the Screening Questionnaire: a Screening Questionnaire for adults who know the child well (Appendix 1) and a Screening Questionnaire for the child (Appendix 2). The latter is simplified and includes pictures to facilitate the comprehension of children with language difficulties.

The Screening Questionnaires will need to be completed prior to the Bridge Meeting by the following parties:

- **Primary school teacher:** In order to screen for the kind of difficulties with which a pupil is most likely to require support within the primary school.

- **Parents/carers:** To provide information about the child's difficulties and strengths which may not be apparent in the school environment, but could be crucial for creating an Individualised Transition Plan for the pupil. Very often pupils with ASD can only express their frustration in a 'safe' home environment.

■ **Child:** This version is for the child to give details about their hopes and worries about transitioning into secondary school.

WHEN SHOULD YOU COMPLETE SCREENING QUESTIONNAIRES?

Screening Questionnaires need to be completed and sent to the allocated professional from the secondary school in preparation for the Bridge Meeting.

Figure P.2 illustrates the process of information gathering and dissemination. It aims to highlight how STEP-ASD is intended to be individualised for each pupil. The first step consists of an initial screening for all potential areas of strength and difficulty, through the use of the Screening Questionnaires (Step 1 and Appendix 1). Therefore it includes a broad range of areas to consider. The Transition Management Plan (Step 3 and Appendix 3) narrows this down and outlines only the relevant areas of strength and difficulty for a particular pupil identified from the Screening Questionnaires. The Transition Management Plan also identifies everyone's roles in supporting the pupil's transition. The Pupil Profile (Step 4 and Appendix 4) is a succinct summary of only the most essential information about the pupil with which all secondary school staff will need to be familiar. It aims to be as concise and user-friendly as possible for busy secondary school professionals.

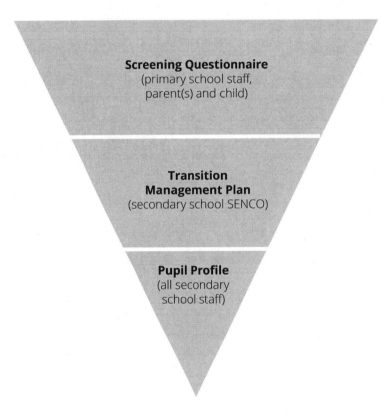

Figure P.2: Process of information gathering and disseminating

Step 2: Bridge Meeting

WHAT IS A BRIDGE MEETING?

A Bridge Meeting between the allocated professionals from both primary and secondary schools, the pupil and their parents/carers is an essential component of successful planning for transition. It provides an opportunity for those most closely involved in supporting the pupil to meet, review the areas of priority support needs identified in the Screening Questionnaires, and devise a Transition Management Plan for the pupil.

WHO SHOULD ATTEND THE BRIDGE MEETING AND WHEN?

The Bridge Meeting should be conducted during the spring term prior to the child's transition and the following parties should be invited:

- Allocated professional from the secondary school

- Allocated professional from the primary school

- Parents/carers of the pupil

- Pupil – whenever possible, the pupil should also be invited to join a part of the meeting at the end, in order to provide them with an opportunity to review the Transition Management Plan and offer their views and wishes.

WHAT IS THE PURPOSE OF THE BRIDGE MEETING?

The purpose of the Bridge Meeting is to:

- **Identify areas of the pupil's support needs:** By reviewing the completed Screening Questionnaires the following support needs should be identified:

    - **Areas of priority need:** All areas in which the primary school teacher and the parents/carers ticked '1' within the Screening Questionnaires. Areas the pupil circled as 'worried' in the Child Screening Questionnaire should be considered for inclusion here, if appropriate.

    - **Areas requiring specific support strategies:** All areas in which the primary school teacher and the parents/carers ticked '2' within the Screening Questionnaires. Areas the pupil circled as 'worried' should be considered for inclusion here, if not addressed within the areas of priority need.

    - **Issues to be aware of:** All areas in which the primary school teacher and the parents/carers ticked '3' within the Screening Questionnaires. Areas the pupil circled as 'worried' could be included here, if there is sufficient evidence that the pupil has a sufficient repertoire of coping strategies in this domain.

- **Identify and agree upon appropriate management and support strategies:**

    - **Areas of priority support needs:** These will require a proactive and consistent management plan (e.g. specific steps to ensure prevention of bullying through multiple measures – introducing a buddy system, 'safe havens' during the highest risk times and adult supervision when needed).

■ **Areas requiring specific support strategies:** These areas do not necessarily require intensive targeting, but the pupil would benefit from a general approach (e.g. shortening of spoken instructions or provision of a visual timetable).

■ **Issues to be aware of:** These include areas which the pupil may not be able to alter and which do not require any specific management, although awareness of which could help to prevent misunderstandings (e.g. teachers may need to be aware that the pupil has difficulty with the use of figures of speech or that what appears to be an inappropriate personal remark may not have any malicious intent behind it).

These strategies can be identified first through the Screening Questionnaires (in which the primary school teacher and the parents/carers have identified previously successful measures) and, second, through Part 2 of the Transition Pack (in which the corresponding management strategies for each area of the questionnaire are outlined). Inviting the pupil's views on what they would find helpful is recommended. However, it might be more helpful to have informal discussions with the pupil prior to the Bridge Meeting, as for some children with ASD, attending meetings and group discussions can be anxiety provoking. A one to one setting with a familiar adult (parent or primary school professional) might facilitate the pupil's ability to express their views more successfully.

■ **Develop a Transition Management Plan and Pupil Profile:** A summary of the discussions about the identified support needs, the agreed management strategies and the action plan, as described below.

Step 3: Transition Management Plan

What is a Transition Management Plan?

The Transition Management Plan is a succinct summary of the identified support needs (depending on the level of their significance), and the agreed action plan detailing who will carry out which management and support strategies. The Transition Management Plan is a working document for everyone involved in supporting the child's transition, outlining how to help the pupil with the transition. Please see Appendix 3 for a copy of the Transition Management Plan.

How to develop a Transition Management Plan

The Transition Management Plan should be developed by the end of the Bridge Meeting, on the basis of the sharing of knowledge of the child, strategies that are known to work and strategies outlined in STEP-ASD. The input of the teacher from the secondary school will be crucial here, in order to ensure the strategies are well adapted to the new environment of the secondary school setting. Consistency of approach is very important for children with ASD, so it is essential to ensure that the agreed plan is workable, applicable in the secondary school setting and transferable across different settings within the school. For example, if a child would benefit from having a copy of a timetable in advance, and if this is not yet available, alternatives can be explored. This could include examples from previous years, a clear explanation to the child of how to read the timetable, and giving them a realistic timeframe of when the actual timetable can be provided.

HOW SHOULD TASKS BE DISTRIBUTED IN THE TRANSITION MANAGEMENT PLAN?

The purpose of scheduling the Bridge Meeting in the spring term is to allow sufficient time for all parties involved to address areas which will help the pupil to transition successfully. Not only will the teachers from the secondary school need time to plan ahead, but the primary school teachers, the parents/carers and the young person themselves will need an opportunity to make the necessary preparations. It is recommended that tasks are distributed according to the following rationale:

- **Allocated professional from the primary school:** The most helpful areas to focus on would include school-based skills, such as work with the pupil on organisational skills and independent use of the timetable, or learning new, more age-appropriate behaviours (e.g. learning that bringing a fluffy toy to the secondary school may not be well received and replacing this habit by a more socially acceptable alternative).

- **Parent/carer:** As it is the parents/carers who spend most time with the child, they can help in many important ways by preparing the child mentally, emotionally and in practical ways (e.g. preparing the pupil for a new journey to school in a gradual way, or helping the child to develop self-management strategies to address an area of difficulty, such as doing up buttons or fastenings on the new uniform).

- **Pupil:** The pupil may need or want to complete their own Transition Workbook (Appendix 24) and familiarise themselves with different aspects of the new school in practical ways (e.g. visiting the secondary school to familiarise themselves with different classrooms or to discover where they could find a quiet area if necessary).

- **Allocated professional from the secondary school:** The essential role for the secondary school professional will be to ensure necessary preparations are made and to take the responsibility for the dissemination of the information gathered at the Bridge Meeting. This takes the form of the Pupil Profile, as outlined below.

Step 4: Pupil PROFILE
WHAT IS A PUPIL PROFILE?

The Pupil Profile is a summary of only the key information that all secondary school staff will need to be familiar with. Whilst the Transition Management Plan included all the different tasks and preparations for the transition, the Pupil Profile outlines only the most essential information and key strategies that will need to be used within the secondary school setting. In practical terms, this means that only the information relevant to the secondary school setting will be included in the Pupil Profile, and strategies agreed for the parents and primary school professionals will remain only in the Transition Management Plan. The aim of the Pupil Profile is to be as concise and user-friendly as possible for busy secondary school professionals, who may have precious little time and capacity to familiarise themselves with more extensive reports about the pupil. Please see Appendix 4 for a copy of the Pupil Profile.

HOW DO YOU DEVELOP A PUPIL PROFILE?

The Pupil Profile should be completed at the end of the Bridge Meeting by the secondary school professional on the basis of the information gathered. It should not require any additional information, as it is only a more succinct form of the Transition Management Plan.

HOW TO USE THE PUPIL PROFILE

The information contained within the Pupil Profile will need to be disseminated amongst all staff at the secondary school, including administrators, janitors and catering staff. It is also important to ensure that any new supply teachers are also provided with a copy of the Pupil Profile to ensure a consistent approach.

FINAL CONSIDERATIONS

This process may seem time consuming but evidence shows that proactive strategies are the most effective way to ensure the child's successful transition to secondary school. Having a proactive plan in place and the opportunity to distribute tasks to all involved parties may help to save a substantial amount of time and resources when a pupil starts attending the new school. Focusing on preventing secondary difficulties associated with ASD can be not only a very effective way of allocating resources, but also a very satisfying process, which will be greatly appreciated by the pupils and their families.

SUMMARY OF PART ONE

Figure P.3 illustrates the process of information gathering and dissemination. It aims to highlight how STEP-ASD is intended to be individualised for each pupil. The first step consists of an initial screening for all potential areas of strength and difficulty through the Screening Questionnaires (Step 1 and Appendices 1 and 2). The Transition Management Plan (Step 3 and Appendix 3) outlines only the relevant areas of the strengths and difficulties for a particular pupil identified from the Screening Questionnaires and everyone's roles in supporting the pupil's transition. The Pupil Profile (Step 4 and Appendix 4) is a succinct summary of only the most essential information about the pupil with which all secondary school staff will need to be familiar. It aims to be as concise and user-friendly as possible for busy secondary school professionals.

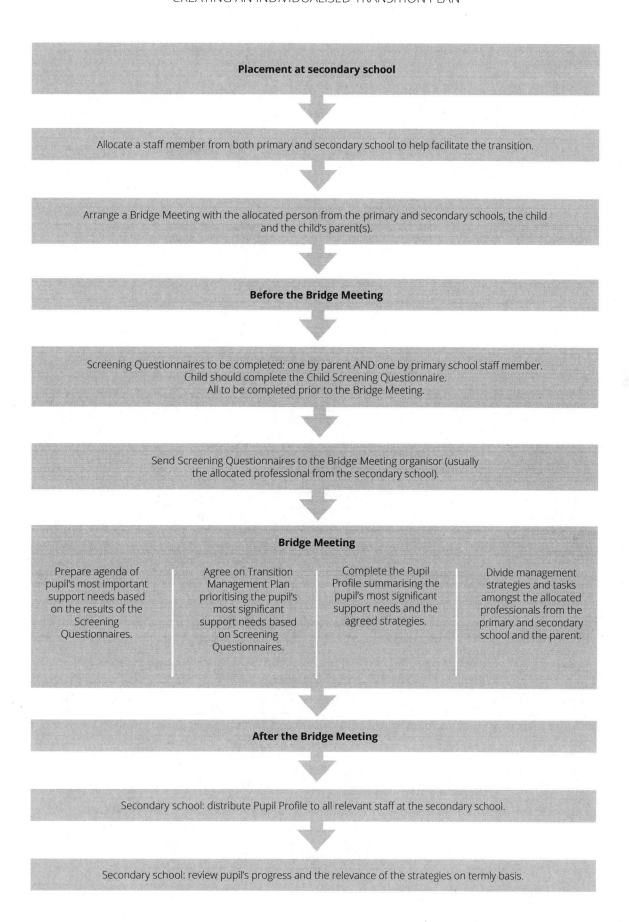

Figure P.3: An overall summary of the implementation of STEP-ASD

PART TWO

RESOURCE CHAPTERS

CHAPTER 1

GENERAL SUPPORT WITH TRANSITION TO SECONDARY SCHOOL

WHY IS THIS IMPORTANT?

Transition to secondary school can be challenging for all children. It is a first major step towards achieving greater independence and many children worry about how they will cope. Children can be insecure about having to make new friends, anxious about getting lost in the new unfamiliar environment, unsure about how they will cope with homework or worried about rumours of bullying.

How do children with ASD experience this challenge? Difficulties with adapting to even minor changes are one of the defining features of their disability. This occurs daily – for example when people change their social plans, when transport fails, when a computer breaks down or when rules of a game suddenly shift. As a result, children with ASD have to deal with increased anxiety on a daily basis. As there are few visible signs of the disability, such as a wheelchair or crutches, this kind of social communication disability may not be immediately apparent.

However, a unique aspect of ASD is that it encompasses special strengths and positive qualities. Whilst difficulty with coping with changes can be very disabling, children with ASD can thrive on clarity and predictability with surprising enthusiasm. Whilst clear rules can be 'something to secretly break' for many typically developing children, pupils with ASD can blossom with these and adhere to them beyond expectations. When they understand what is expected of them, pupils with ASD can go to great lengths to try to meet these expectations.

HOW CAN WE HELP?

Children with ASD can vary greatly in the amount of individualised support they may require. Some children may come to secondary school with a Statement of Special Educational Needs, which will provide for their one-to-one support needs. Others may not require such intensive support. However, most pupils with ASD benefit greatly from clarity and predictability. It is therefore important to think through the general issues the pupil may benefit from prior to familiarisation. What follows is a list of strategies from which pupils with ASD often benefit. Not every pupil will require all of the strategies listed. The importance and benefits of each area will be highlighted in the Screening Questionnaires and can be further discussed at the Bridge Meeting. If it is agreed that it would be helpful for the pupil to have a special project to work on in familiarising themselves with the new school, most of the suggestions below are also included in a child-friendly form in the child's Transition Workbook (Appendix 24), which is a practical workbook for pupils.

Allocated adult

Most children with ASD benefit greatly from knowing that there is an identified adult who can be approached if needed. Some pupils with ASD may need to utilise this support only occasionally, at the time of significant need. But having clear reassurance that this support is available, if needed, can be a source of great comfort to virtually all children on the autism spectrum. Providing this support is one of the most helpful strategies any school can implement.

- **Identifying an appropriate adult:** In choosing the appropriate person to be the allocated adult, perhaps the most important aspect to consider is availability. Whilst SENCOs tend to have the most in-depth knowledge of ASD, their demands and multiple roles may not allow them to provide space for individualised support. In most large schools their role can be therefore utilised much more effectively by supporting a person with a greater availability with the necessary information about the pupil, their support needs and ASD in general. The roles of the 'allocated adult' can be often successfully performed by form tutors, SEN assistants or LSAs, who may have more frequent contact and involvement with the pupil, as well as greater availability.

- **Familiarisation with the allocated adult:** Children with ASD tend to benefit greatly from being able to meet a person whom they could approach if needed in the new unfamiliar environment prior to their transition. Depending on the child, even one or two brief meetings with an allocated adult during the child's visits can be a significant source of reassurance. However, the degree of opportunity for familiarisation will have to be adjusted to each pupil individually, as some children may need to meet the person more often.

- **Clarification of the contact with the allocated adult:** Children with ASD may often require very specific instructions in order to be able to utilise the available support appropriately. Even if they have been introduced to the person they can approach for help, many pupils will need specific guidance about the times and places they can be approached (e.g. during break times or during specified brief times in their timetable).

Gradual familiarisation

- **Visits to the school:** Children with ASD tend to benefit greatly from gradual visits and opportunities to familiarise themselves with a new environment. If helpful and possible, these visits could be facilitated by an LSA or even a parent/carer of the child prior to the transition.

- **Secondary workbook:** Many children with ASD can process information best when they are in a calm, quiet and undisturbed environment. Some children with ASD also tend to seek reassurance repetitively. Having a 'workbook' about the secondary school can be extremely useful, as this enables parents/carers to support the child over the summer holidays and enhances the benefits of the gradual visits. This can take the form of a school prospectus or an opportunity to take photographs of the different areas of the school during the visits. Making such a booklet can be time consuming in the first instance, but it can then be re-used with small adjustments for future pupils with ASD. Alternatively, if no resources are available, parents/carers can be encouraged to take the initiative, which is likely to be met with great enthusiasm. Agreeing on a special project, which could be conducted with support from the primary school staff, might also be another helpful solution.

- **School rules:** Each school usually has a specific code of behaviour, which most children tend to pick up very quickly. However, understanding 'unspoken rules' can be extremely difficult for most children with ASD. It might be useful to think about any significant changes in school rules between primary and secondary school, and 'spell them out' for the child well in advance. This would enable the child to work on getting used to the new expectations and on altering their behaviour over time, if needed, prior to starting in the new school.

- **Staff pictures:** As children with ASD tend to have significant difficulty with meeting new people, having photographs of staff members can help parents/carers and primary school staff to support the child to familiarise themselves with new secondary school staff. This would enable the child to feel a lot more comfortable, as well as more secure prior to these first encounters.

Orientation

- **School map:** Visual-spatial skills are a strong feature for many children with ASD, although many of them can have significant difficulty with self-organisation. Providing a map of the school for children with ASD will therefore enable them to familiarise themselves with different locations in the building. This will in turn help to reduce demands on self-organisation once they are required to arrive at the right place in time for lessons.

- **Timetable:** Due to their significant difficulty with organising themselves, most children with ASD could benefit greatly from an opportunity to familiarise themselves with the timetable. This can prevent many difficulties, such as the pupil being late, lost, or anxious.

- **Colour coding and matching:** Many children with ASD have good visual skills which can be used to help them with their organisational difficulties. If the school map, timetable and pictures of staff members can be obtained, parents/carers or the allocated adult (often a SENCO, TA, LSA, class teacher or form tutor) from the primary school can help the child to colour code different areas of the new school and match them to different subjects and teachers. This can be a very successful strategy in fostering the independence of children with ASD prior to them starting secondary school.

- **Safe havens:** For children with ASD and comorbid high levels of anxiety, sensory sensitivities, repetitive interests or a history of being bullied, having the reassurance of a secure place, where they can calm down, seek security, reduce sensory overload, or perform rituals they need to carry out in private can prove invaluable. Highlighting a secure and private place which can be available to the pupil if needed can therefore be very important for some children.

- **Sensitive locations:** Some children with ASD can be very sensitive to, or particularly vulnerable in specific environments. For example, some children may find canteens and meal times overwhelming due to their sensory over-sensitivity to sound or smells. Other children may be anxious about locating toilets in different areas of the school if they have difficulties with orientation. Thinking about proactive solutions, such as allocating the most suitable alternative locations, or highlighting different places on the school map can help prevent many possible difficulties.

Sharing of ASD diagnosis

Discussing this issue with the parents/carers and the pupil prior to the transition is very important, as some management strategies in the following chapters are adjusted differently, depending on the parent/carer and child's wishes about disclosure of the diagnosis. It would therefore be beneficial to share the information provided here and in the appendices (Appendix 21) in order to help the parents/carers and the child reach an informed decision and gain clarity about how to proceed once the child moves to secondary school.

- **Discussing the diagnosis with the child:** This is often a question parents/carers think about a lot. Many parents/carers ask when is the right time to explain the diagnosis of ASD to the child, what to say and how to say it, or wonder if they should talk about it at all. Many parents/carers worry that learning about the diagnosis will impact on the child's self-esteem or upset them. However, as children become older and approach secondary school age, they often start noticing that they do certain things differently. This is certainly an important age to consider this issue. Whilst many parents/carers worry about the impact of the 'label' on the child, children have a need to make sense of their difference. A lack of information can often result in children finding different and often unhelpful 'labels' such as that they are 'stupid', 'bad' or 'weird', which can have a detrimental impact on their self-esteem. Knowing about their diagnosis can also help the child to learn to manage their difficulties more effectively, learn about their strengths and to find a support group if they wish (for example, through meeting other young people with ASD, joining AS forums, etc.).

If this issue is of interest to the parents/carers and the child, please see Appendix 21 for further details.

- **Sharing the diagnosis with others:** Parents/carers frequently try to weigh up the pros and cons of sharing the child's diagnosis with others, especially peers. Parents/carers often worry that their child would be stigmatised by their peers if they knew about the diagnosis. At the same time, if the peer group does not have an insight into the nature and reasons for the child's unique way of thinking and being, peers may not be as understanding and supportive as they could be if they had known. However, other children will pick up on certain differences. Thinking of some form of explanation that parents/carers and the child will be happy for teachers to use to explain their behaviour is therefore very important. This matter should be decided between the child and parents/carers. Appendix 21 provides helpful guidance and advice on the different points to consider.

Peer support

Children with ASD often experience anxiety about meeting new people, especially peers. If there is another child with ASD who will also be transitioning, it might be very helpful to arrange for them to meet, for example during one of the visits. Alternatively, if there are any children from the primary school transitioning to the same secondary school, it might be helpful for the staff to facilitate a supportive friendship between them (see Chapter 2, Social Interaction). Knowing at least some peers can help to reduce children's anxiety about being left alone on the first day.

Travel to the new school

A new journey to school can be a big concern for some families with a child with ASD, and it can be useful to think about this issue well in advance, in order to allow plenty of time for them to practise the route. Many children find independent travelling so difficult and anxiety provoking that this can impact on their wellbeing even before they arrive at school. For other children, the journey to school can be particularly worrying due to the risk of bullying, which often occurs during unsupervised times. If this is the case, thinking of alternative strategies such as finding a 'travel buddy' in the neighbourhood can be very reassuring.

First day in the new school

Even when well prepared, some children with ASD can have such significant anxiety that they worry about being lost or alone, or panic about having a 'meltdown' in front of everyone on the first day. Some children can be reassured greatly by being welcomed by someone they have met previously upon arrival on their first day of school. A low level of support in having someone who could help direct them to the right place if needed can be very beneficial.

Individual support needs

Specific support needs, personalised for each pupil, can be identified from the Screening Questionnaires and during the Bridge Meeting. Relevant chapters in the resource pack will, we hope, provide helpful preventative and management strategies, which can be implemented proactively by the parents/carers, pupil or the school professionals. An example of a specific support need can be seen in the case of homework, which tends to be troublesome for various reasons for most pupils with ASD. Proactive identification of these issues would be beneficial for the secondary school professionals:

- **Homework:** Whilst pupils with ASD tend to benefit from familiarisation with rules, adherence to which is important for most, homework can be a very sensitive issue. This is usually not due to a pupil's reluctance to comply with the assignments, even if it may appear to be the case, but instead there may be underlying reasons for not being able to do so, such as difficulties with being organised, with working memory or the ability to note homework down, or due to specific learning difficulties.

  Addressing this issue in advance can prevent many disappointments on the side of the teaching staff, as well as frustration for the pupil and their family. If this may be the case, please view Chapter 6 (Planning and Organisation Problems) and Appendix 20 for further details.

 FINAL CONSIDERATIONS

A proactive approach to helping children with ASD to familiarise themselves with the new environment, people and expectations can significantly reduce the child's stress levels. It can also help prevent many difficulties after starting in the new school and increase the likelihood of a positive new start. Even if the school resources for this kind of preparatory work are limited, most families and pupils with ASD will be motivated to work on the above strategies themselves and will appreciate the opportunity to do so. Furthermore, preparing for the transition and empowering the parents/carers and the pupil to implement the strategies would help to set up a positive collaborative relationship between the family and the school, as well as enhance a pupil's initiative.

CHAPTER 2

SOCIAL INTERACTION

WHY IS THIS IMPORTANT?

Social skills are essential aspects of a child's functioning. Social skills are not only important for building friendships and ensuring social integration, but are also vital for effective collaboration, teamwork and constructive cooperation. Learning social skills is a fundamental developmental task to ensure successful functioning within society.

In addition, social integration is also very important for our emotional wellbeing. Research shows that children without friends are at significantly increased risk of developing low self-esteem or depression, or being victims of bullying. Difficulties with making friends can have long-lasting effects on relationships and employment.

Schools are crucial in our society for helping children to acquire appropriate social skills and behaviours, alongside learning academic and practical skills. It is a combination of both of those sets of skills that prepares children for the future.

WHAT DO WE NEED TO KNOW ABOUT SOCIAL INTERACTION?

Learning social skills

Social skills allow us to relate to and socialise with others. Social skills develop through observing and modelling others and through implicit learning. Making friends comes very naturally and intuitively for typically developing children, but a child with ASD will have to learn social rules at an intellectual level. Tony Attwood, an ASD expert from Australia, explained this process as being similar to learning a foreign language (Attwood, 2004).

School is an optimal place to build on social skills and develop shared play for most typically developing children, because it provides continuous opportunities for social interaction. However, the complex social environment of schools can be extremely overwhelming and confusing for many pupils with ASD.

Social difficulties in ASD

Impairments in social interaction skills are one of the defining diagnostic features of ASD. However, these difficulties can be varied and present very differently in each child. Whilst some children might have unusual or reduced eye contact, others have problems initiating interactions, understanding verbal and nonverbal social cues, initiating and maintaining conversations and understanding unwritten social rules. Pupils with ASD can have difficulties with empathy, that is, 'putting themselves in someone else's shoes' or with understanding social context and hence act in an inappropriate way unintentionally. For example, the child with ASD might memorise a friend's joke but repeat it in a different, more formal context, where it can be perceived as being rude or challenging. However, children with ASD rarely intend to hurt someone else's feelings and would be very upset to learn about it.

Myths about ASD – lonely or loner?

Researchers and health professionals alike used to think that children with difficulties on the autism spectrum desire and choose to be alone (Kanner, 1943). We now understand that this is a gross oversimplification. Several studies have found that children with ASD do indeed feel *lonely*, much more so than their peers. Whilst some children with ASD may prefer engaging in solitary activities, many children often have the social desire, but don't know how to initiate and maintain friendships.

 # HOW CAN WE HELP?

Pupils with ASD are often very keen to learn appropriate social skills and to make friends. Two sections below detail strategies to promote social understanding and social inclusion:

- **Proactive strategies:** Promoting social understanding

- **Management strategies:** Promoting social inclusion.

Proactive strategies: promoting social understanding

- **Direct instruction**
  Direct instruction is a good way to develop social peer group participation and social communication. It helps to provide steps required to build social skills and presents an opportunity to practise them. Direct instructions are based on the principle that children with ASD are very good at following rules (Frankel & Myatt, 2003).

  - **Turn-taking:** Some pupils with ASD struggle with taking turns (e.g. in conversation), which can lead to frustration for their peers and teachers. Turn-taking rules can be taught explicitly with the help of visual cue cards or comic strips (see Appendix 6).

- **Rules in conversation**: Pupils who struggle to initiate conversations or to know the appropriate time and place for a certain topic benefit from learning concrete conversational rules. It has been shown to be helpful to have a visual list of these rules accessible and it is important to practise these in real conversations (see Appendix 7).

- **Rules when entering a group**: A proportion of pupils with ASD have difficulty with correctly interpreting nonverbal cues. It is fundamental to understand these cues in order to know when to approach a group of peers and how. Children with ASD have been known to benefit from remembering concrete rules of group entry, as outlined in the appendices (see Appendix 7).

- **Social Stories**

  A Social Story™ is a technique used to explain socially appropriate or desirable behaviour in a consistent visual form and has been found to be effective for pupils with ASD (created by Carol Gray; see Appendix 8). There is a general consistent format of how to write and use Social Stories, which children with ASD become accustomed to. It explains social cues and appropriate student responses in a specific situation.

  Social Stories should be used to explain a situation from the child's perspective and at a cognitive and age-appropriate level. The advantage of Social Stories is that they can be adapted to a variety of social situations and behaviours, such as:

  - Explaining reasons for behaviour of others

  - Teaching situation-specific social skills

  - Introducing changes and new routines.

Prepared stories can be found in Carol Gray's Social Stories books or adapted according to the child's specific need (Gray, 1994, 2010).

- **Social skills groups**

  Social skills groups, in which children with ASD or other social or communication difficulties can learn and practise a range of social skills, are often a very popular way of promoting social understanding and positive prosocial behaviours. In particular, the group format can decrease extraneous demands on limited resources, whilst it in addition provides very helpful opportunities to practise learned skills in a safe environment. However, the group's coherence can sometimes pose a challenge as children's level of social difficulties and cognitive potential can vary so significantly. Paying attention to the selection of group members is therefore important. Although social skills groups can be helpful, it is important to highlight that their benefit can be limited, unless children are learning gender- and age-appropriate behaviours, which would be accepted by their peers. Group facilitators should be aware that socially acceptable behaviours for teenage boys vary significantly from those of girls, or adults (e.g. teaching a teenage boy to look someone right into their eyes can be perceived provocatively rather than a sign of them listening intently). There is a wide range of resources available to help structure social skills groups in schools. To name just a few: PEERS (Laugeson & Frankel, 2010), Children's Friendship Training (Frankel & Myatt, 2003) and Social Skills Training (Baker, 2003).

Management strategies: promoting social inclusion

- **Structured social groups**

  Pupils with ASD benefit from structured activities as they struggle to know what to say or do in different social situations or how to initiate a social activity. Organising structured lunch time or after-school clubs are a great opportunity for the children to meet and integrate with like-minded pupils, enabling social inclusion and potential friendships. There can be different formats of structured social groups:

  - **Peer network** (Garrison-Harrell, Kamps & Kravits, 1997): The aim is to organise social, not academic activities, based on common interests in the school environment (e.g. IT or chess), which take place regularly at the same times and on the same days. It is an opportunity to promote age-appropriate interactions and possibly even friendships. Children are encouraged to join the group whenever they wish, and pupils with ASD may often require an adult to introduce them to the group or the club. Although an adult supervises the group, the roles of each child do not have to be specifically structured, unless the child appears at a loss as to how to join in.

  - **Teamwork:** This is a group which aims to promote positive prosocial behaviours via collaborative joint activity. This group, or possibly just a dyad, is set up in relation to a certain project (e.g. science, practical DIY or volunteering project). These groups are supervised by an adult, but the roles of each child are often more clearly defined based on their contribution towards the project. These groups are suitable for children with ASD who are socially withdrawn and find social activities and joining groups anxiety-provoking. Such teamwork can also have a very positive effect on self-esteem as it provides the child with an opportunity to make a valued contribution.

- **Peer mediation**

  In peer mediation, typically developing and socially skilled pupils are encouraged to help their peers with ASD to develop social skills in a natural setting. This can be a helpful strategy to increase inclusion via the following formats:

  - **Buddy system:** The aim of this intervention is to identify socially competent children in the classroom who have a natural rapport with the child with ASD and can aid the child in the classroom, playground and in social situations. It is particularly helpful if the buddies are sociable and popular. Sometimes sensitive advice from peers about what to wear and talk about is more readily accepted than from adults. Also the buddies are present in situations where adults are not. The buddy can, for example, help with the following areas:

    - Teaching classroom routines (e.g. where to put homework, what to do when you first arrive for class, where to put materials)

    - Getting the child with ASD involved in conversation with other children in free time

    - Helping with the timetable and possibly showing them to the next class (e.g. guiding them through hallway).

Things to consider when setting up a buddy system:

- It is important to pick more than one child to be a buddy to a child with ASD to enable the buddies to take turns so that they do not feel overwhelmed by the responsibility or do not feel that their own opportunities to engage with other children are limited.

- In order to facilitate longer-term, positive relationships between the buddies, it is helpful to consider which relationships can be mutually beneficial. For example, the child with ASD who excels in academic work can be paired up with a socially sensitive and skilled child who may struggle academically, so that both pupils can support each other in reciprocal ways.

- The buddy system also has benefits for teachers and the child chosen as a buddy. Teachers may need to give less support to the child with ASD who has a buddy in class, especially during the non-structured times. Additionally, several studies have shown that the child who is acting as the buddy experiences enhanced personal growth and greater awareness of disability issues. However, it is important to ensure that the buddies receive regular recognition and praise from the teacher, which very strongly reinforces their motivation.

- **Circle of Friends:** This is a strategy which is based on a group of volunteers (6–8 volunteers) who meet regularly with the child with ASD and an adult facilitator to discuss the challenges the child with ASD faces (Frederickson, Warren & Turner, 2005). This provides a very helpful opportunity for the child to receive practical and emotional support from their peers, during and beyond the session. During each session, a particular problem is discussed and children can brainstorm different strategies and solutions as well as suggest ways in which they will contribute to helping the child to resolve it (see Appendix 9).

CAUTION

Things to consider when setting up a buddy system

It is essential to carefully ensure issues of confidentiality, boundaries and security of the group for the child with ASD. Unless skillfully facilitated there are risks that the child may end up feeling even more rejected or be teased should any sensitive information be disclosed. If you are interested in further information about how to run Circle of Friends please refer to Appendix 9.

Children with ASD are at a high risk of exploitation due to their social naivety. Often they are so highly motivated to fit in that they are easily cajoled into inappropriate situations or behaviours, hoping that this will make them popular. Children with ASD may not realise that they are being misled. It is not unknown for children with ASD to engage in anti-social or other inappropriate behaviours, having been promised by others that this will make them 'cool'. Having some true friends or caring buddies can be a strong protective factor for these socially vulnerable pupils.

FINAL CONSIDERATIONS

Remembering and helping other children to understand that behaviours which may at times appear inappropriate and unusual are a result of the pupil's genuine social difficulties associated with their diagnosis can help prevent misinterpretation of the pupil's actions (e.g. perceiving direct and literal statements as intentionally hurtful). Whilst pupils with ASD have difficulties with social understanding and social interaction, they are often highly motivated to fit in and to make friends. Helping typically developing children to appreciate the pupil's strengths and positive qualities (e.g. loyalty, truthfulness, reliability) and finding opportunities for the pupil with ASD to engage with their peers and form friendships will not only assist greatly in furthering their social skills, but will also contribute significantly to their emotional wellbeing and enjoyment from being at school. This effort will also be greatly appreciated by the parents/carers of children with ASD, for whom their child's emotional wellbeing at school is of paramount importance, often surpassing any academic hopes for the child.

CHAPTER 3

LANGUAGE DIFFICULTIES

WHY IS THIS IMPORTANT?

Impairment of verbal communication (sometimes referred to as a 'language impairment') is one of the key diagnostic features of ASD. Children with ASD have difficulty with the comprehension and/or use of language. Even very bright children with adult-sounding vocabularies can have less obvious, idiosyncratic difficulties in their verbal communication.

Research indicates that children with language impairment in the context of ASD are chronically at risk of underperforming academically. Furthermore, the presence of a language impairment will often have a negative impact on their emotional wellbeing. Owing to their language difficulties, this group of children are more likely than others to experience poor mental health (e.g. anxiety disorders, low self-esteem or challenging behaviour). They are also more at risk of being excluded by peers and bullied.

This chapter focuses on helping children with ASD to overcome the potentially negative consequences of their language impairments on their academic performance and other areas of their lives. By using strategies aimed at managing or compensating for the child's language difficulties, school staff can help to prevent and overcome these adverse effects.

WHAT DO WE NEED TO KNOW ABOUT LANGUAGE DIFFICULTIES?

Learning to understand and use language

Children's language development is core to their ability to understand and interpret what is happening around them, as well as their ability to engage in interaction with others.

From infancy, typically developing children learn to understand and to talk by listening to those around them. This continues into adolescence and beyond. For children with ASD this process is not so straightforward and often takes a different or delayed course. Their impairments in areas such as social interaction and imagination (as identified in the dyad, previously known as a triad, of impairments referred to in Part 1 of this pack) mean that they are slow to develop the prerequisite 'building blocks' for the development of language, such as attention and listening skills, turn-taking skills and symbolic play skills. Conversely, many children with ASD develop language at an appropriate or advanced rate in the first years of their lives, but are often noted at a later stage to have qualitative difficulties in how they understand and use language.

Language difficulties in ASD

There is a considerable range in the type and nature of language difficulties seen in children with ASD. At one end of this range is the group of children who have a marked difficulty following spoken directions, understanding vocabulary and using words and sentences. At the other, however, is the group of children most frequently encountered by teachers in mainstream schools, namely those who are of average or above-average intellectual ability. These children will typically have what are sometimes considered to be subtle language difficulties, such as a tendency to 'take things literally', use language in an overly formal or idiosyncratic way or have difficulty making 'small talk'. It is important to note here that children with ASD can have a scattered profile of linguistic strengths and weaknesses, however, and a child's good performance in one area (e.g. excellent or even advanced vocabulary) should not necessarily be taken to indicate strong language skills in all domains.

- **Receptive language impairment**
  The term 'receptive language difficulty' (sometimes called 'receptive language impairment') refers to problems understanding spoken language. Children with receptive language impairment are likely to struggle with linguistic aspects such as following spoken directions, understanding different sentence structures or comprehending the meaning of specific words or concepts.

- **Expressive language impairment**
  The term 'expressive language difficulty' (sometimes called 'expressive language impairment') refers to problems using words and sentences. Children with expressive language impairment have difficulty with aspects such as structuring their sentences (e.g. tending to jumble the word order), using grammatical markers (e.g. using immature grammatical forms) or naming items.

- **Figurative/idiosyncraticlanguage difficulties**
  In addition to the receptive and expressive language difficulties mentioned above, children with ASD who are of average or above-average cognitive ability may display more subtle language features. One such feature is a tendency to be overly literal in their interpretation of language. This will affect their comprehension of aspects of language which can have multiple meanings, such as idioms, metaphors and jokes.

  Expressively, this group of children will also have difficulty taking the social context into account (e.g. an oral presentation to the class versus a chat with a classmate) and may use overly formal or pedantic words which can sound socially odd. Children with ASD may also present with 'stereotyped language' whereby they repeat a turn of phrase heard elsewhere (e.g. conversation between adults) out of context, again marking the child out as different socially. Although these kinds of difficulties with language could be considered 'subtle', the personal, social and academic consequences can be considerable.

- **Children with intellectual disability/general learning difficulties**

  Children with ASD whose overall intellectual ability is below average or is in the general learning difficulties range will, by definition, experience difficulty learning to understand and/or use language. However, these difficulties will often be commensurate with their nonverbal (more visually based) reasoning skills. Whilst these children might not, therefore, be expected to 'catch up' with their peers in the area of language, the strategies described below will nonetheless be useful in facilitating their comprehension and expression.

- **Specific language impairment**

  Children with a specific language impairment (SLI) profile in the context of their ASD are those whose receptive and/or expressive language skills are significantly weaker than their nonverbal reasoning skills. Typically, the nonverbal reasoning skills of the child with SLI will be age appropriate but their language skills will show a moderate or severe degree of impairment. They may display language features which are atypical rather than simply immature (e.g. unusual word order in sentences). Children with SLI (sometimes called 'specific language disorder', SLD) experience marked difficulties with language which do not show an improvement with generalised language help and they will often require intensive speech and language therapy in order to make progress.

How can we recognise a language impairment?

Difficulties with language comprehension and expression in children with ASD may not always be immediately obvious. However, their effects on academic performance, behaviour and social interaction are likely to be more noticeable. The following are some examples which may be encountered in the classroom:

Example: A usually conscientious child fails to follow spoken directions.

Possible cause: The child is experiencing difficulty remembering and understanding what was said.

Example: A child acts as 'class clown', distracting the teacher's attention to avoid writing an essay.

Possible cause: The child is afraid of failure owing to a difficulty structuring sentences.

Example: When asked in PE class: 'Can you find a partner?' a child appears cheeky in replying, 'yes' but failing to move.

Possible cause: The child has interpreted the indirect request in a literal fashion. The direction, 'Go and find a partner' would be more likely to produce the desired response.

Many other examples will be apparent in a classroom setting. If in doubt as to whether the child with ASD is struggling in the area of language it is best to err on the side of caution and implement the language strategies described in this chapter, while monitoring progress over time. Consultation with a speech and language therapist or psychologist will be useful for children whose difficulties have not been formally assessed.

HOW CAN WE HELP?

There are a number of ways in which we can facilitate and promote the understanding and use of language in children with ASD. Two sections below are advice sections, consisting of:

- **Proactive strategies:** These are general strategies we can implement to help children with ASD in the classroom setting.

- **Management strategies:** These are specific adaptations or activities to facilitate the comprehension and use of language.

Proactive strategies: general strategies for the classroom

- **Strategies for facilitating the comprehension and use of language**

  - **Modifying your own use of language:** Children with ASD will frequently fail to respond appropriately to directions from adults because the language loading in the instructions is too complex. This can result in difficulty following the lesson and off-task or challenging behaviour. Doing the following can help the child to understand:

    - Call the child by name before giving instructions

    - Shorten your spoken sentences

    - Simplify the vocabulary you use (e.g. 'all over the world' rather than 'international'), or briefly explain the meaning of new terms (e.g. 'photosynthesis means...')

    - Slow down your rate of speech

    - Give one part of an instruction at a time

    - Check for understanding (e.g. ask the child to repeat what they are expected to do but make sure that they are not simply repeating verbatim without comprehending)

    - Repeat spoken directions (once or twice)

    - Allow plenty of silence and pause after each instruction (to provide extra time for spoken instructions to be processed)

    - Write down instructions as well as saying them aloud

    - Whenever possible, repeat group instructions individually to the child with ASD.

  - **Facilitating the child's use of language:** There are a number of strategies and techniques we can implement to assist children in learning to use language:

    - Rather than correcting children's use of language, model the target version for them (e.g. if a child with expressive language impairment says, 'The girl runned in the race…she falled on the floor and hurt her,' the teacher might echo: 'Oh really? The woman who ran in the race fell on the ground and hurt herself?').

  ▪ Use comments as well as questions. This encourages conversation, while reducing the perceived pressure for the child to respond.

  ▪ If a child has difficulty naming items, offer a forced choice of two words and put the target word last (e.g. 'Is it a staple or a paperclip you need?'). The word will therefore be the most recent in the child's auditory memory and is more likely to be remembered in the longer term.

▪ **Supporting children who have figurative language difficulties:** Children's literal interpretation or idiosyncratic use of words can sometimes cause their behaviour in the classroom to be mistakenly perceived as cheeky or challenging. This can lead to a breakdown in communication with the child or worse, a sanction being given arising from a language difficulty over which the child has no control. The following is therefore recommended:

  ▪ It is important to raise awareness of the child's ASD diagnosis and language difficulties amongst all school staff (and where appropriate, other pupils). A good rule of thumb is to give the 'benefit of the doubt' (i.e. it is important that school staff realise that it is highly unlikely that the child with ASD is deliberately answering back or being obstinate).

  ▪ In the classroom setting avoid the use of sarcasm as the words are likely to be taken literally by a child with ASD.

  ▪ When you notice yourself using a new figure of speech, try to remember to explain its meaning, at least for the first couple of times you use it (e.g. 'Let's play it by ear – which means that we'll decide tomorrow if we have time to go to the football match').

Management strategies: specific adaptations for the pupil with ASD

As mentioned above, management strategies are specific adaptations or activities to facilitate the comprehension or use of language. The following will largely be relevant for children with moderate/severe language impairments in the context of ASD, or for children of higher ability whose difficulties with figurative language impact greatly on their learning and social interaction. Many strategies would best be implemented on a one-to-one basis by a teaching assistant/learning support assistant or indeed the class teacher.

▪ **Strategies to facilitate the comprehension and use of language**

  ▪ **Use visual strengths to facilitate comprehension:** Children with ASD tend to learn in a different way to their typically developing peers. A common feature is that their nonverbal/visual processing skills are stronger than their language skills. It makes sense, therefore, to use visual strategies to facilitate their understanding and use of language. Whereas the spoken word lasts only a fraction of a second, visual presentation of materials allows the child additional time to process new information and can be referred to while working in class. This might include the following:

- Using handouts with step-by-step instructions for classwork tasks

- Using diagrams, flowcharts or other pictures to illustrate new ideas covered in class

- Extra teaching of key vocabulary and concepts needed for particular subjects (e.g. science/maths/geography) using a visual representation technique such as mind mapping (Buzan, 2002).

- **Encourage children to monitor their own comprehension of language:** Children with ASD will often wish to 'fit in' with their peer group and will not wish to draw attention to their difficulties with language. They will, therefore, have difficulty asking for help when they need it in class. Agree in advance an inconspicuous way for children to indicate that they have difficulty understanding presented tasks (e.g. they may wish to place a bookmark at the side of the desk or write their question down rather than asking it aloud).

- **Encourage the pupil to use language:** Teach the appropriate structure of written language exercises such as essays (introduction, body of essay and conclusion). Teach the need to structure written and spoken narratives (e.g. characters need to be introduced at the beginning, information regarding what happens to them comes in the middle, and the story concludes at the end).

- **Supporting children who have figurative language difficulties**

- **Non-literal language:** Teach pupils the multiple meanings of common figures of speech, such as the meaning of idioms, metaphors or verbal jokes (e.g. 'out of the blue'; 'over the moon'; 'hit the roof', etc.). Remember that multiple meanings of different words may have to be taught separately across various social settings because children with ASD may fail to generalise this knowledge spontaneously.

- Whenever possible, you should represent the multiple meanings in a visual form and discuss these drawings or representations with the child. The following resources involve the visual representation of multiple meanings and are therefore particularly useful for children with ASD:

  - Carol Gray's Social Stories™ involve the drawing of stick figure facial expressions alongside each possible meaning of a non-literal phrase in order to teach the multiple meanings of idioms, metaphors and jokes.

  - The book, *What did you say? What did you mean?* (Welton & Telford, 2004) involves the use of illustrations to demonstrate the interpretation of figures of speech, alongside a simple written explanation for each one.

- **Informal use of language:** Teachers can help children to identify the difference between formal and informal language contexts. It may be useful to do this by giving the child two sheets of paper marked 'formal' and 'informal' and writing down the different language forms appropriate to each one (e.g. 'Good afternoon' might be an appropriate greeting for the school principal but 'hi' is what is said between children).

 ## FINAL CONSIDERATIONS

It is worth remembering that children with ASD may have a good aptitude for many school subjects but will be unable to realise this potential without appropriate personalisation of the curriculum. Adapting strategies, such as modifying one's own use of language, may seem daunting initially, but their use can quickly become habitual.

It can be surprising too in the company of children with ASD to realise just how many phrases with multiple meanings we use in everyday speech and what an opaque language English can be!

It has been noted by some who work in this field that 'good teaching for children with ASD is simply good teaching'. The strategies outlined in this chapter will not only facilitate the understanding and use of language for children with ASD, but they will aid learning for those with a range of additional educational needs in addition to their typically developing peers.

CHAPTER 4

DIFFICULTIES WITH IMAGINATION AND FLEXIBLE THINKING

WHY IS THIS IMPORTANT?

One area of the triad of impairments experienced by children with ASD consists of difficulties with imagination and flexible thinking. Teachers might notice, for example, that some children with ASD may talk at length on topics of great interest only to them or be overly reliant on following exactly the same routine each day at school. This aspect of ASD can impact strongly on children's academic performance, as well as their behaviour in the classroom and their social interaction with peers and teachers. Difficulties with imagination and flexible thinking can manifest themselves in a number of ways, but as with all of the features of ASD there will be considerable variation in the nature and severity of such characteristics in individual children.

The picture is not entirely negative, however. Some aspects of this area of the triad of impairments can be viewed as strengths. For example, many children with ASD value consistency and structure in a way that makes them very reliable and trustworthy. Equally, the ability to sustain focused attention on a particular topic can be an asset when completing schoolwork. Furthermore, some children with ASD can become an 'expert' in their area of special interest. With the appropriate support, the area of interest may even form the basis for a future career.

WHAT DO WE NEED TO KNOW ABOUT DIFFICULTIES WITH IMAGINATION AND FLEXIBLE THINKING?

Learning to understand difficulties with imagination and flexible thinking

Most children with an autism spectrum disorder experience some difficulties with imagination and flexibility of thought. However, as we can see from Figure 4.1 on the following page, this underlying impairment in ASD can present itself in a number of different ways. This chapter aims to help education staff to identify behaviours arising from underlying difficulties with imagination and/or flexibility, and to minimise the problems which they can cause. It is especially important to recognise that, like all of us, children with ASD become especially inflexible when they are feeling anxious or angry. The resulting behaviour can serve various functions for the child, and is best thought of as a coping strategy. Children's difficulty with imagination can compound their inflexibility of thought, since the child has trouble envisaging what is likely to come next in a given situation.

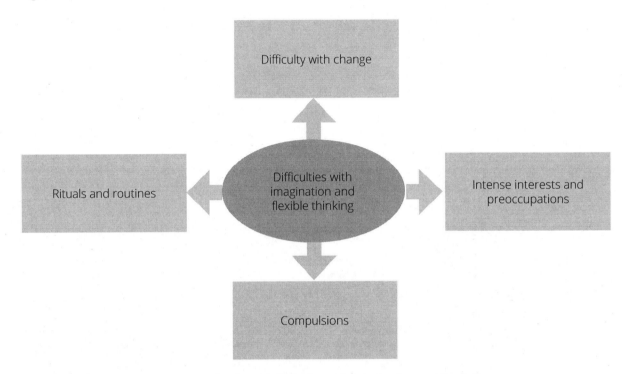

Figure 4.1: The types of difficulty with imagination and flexibility of thought experienced by children with ASD

As we can see from Figure 4.1, children with ASD can experience difficulties with imagination and flexible thinking which can be grouped into four broad categories. These categories of difficulty will be defined below, along with some examples of how each one might present itself in school.

Difficulty with change

The world can be a confusing, stressful place for some children with ASD due to their inflexibility of thought and their need for consistency. It has been suggested that owing to their lack of imagination it is difficult for them to predict what is going to happen next. For this reason, these children have a preference for sameness and routine. Even seemingly minor changes at school (e.g. a change of teacher, cancellation of a scheduled activity or taking a different route to school) can cause upset and distress and can at times lead to challenging behaviour. A school-based example might be the child who becomes highly anxious upon hearing that a substitute teacher will be taking the class for that day. As a way of coping with this anxiety a child with an intense interest in football might spend the lesson writing a list of everyone who has captained Everton FC, rather than completing the work set by the teacher.

Intense interests and preoccupations

Some children with ASD will display an interest in particular topics or items which may seem unusual in their nature and intensity. Particular interests can vary over the course of childhood and into adolescence (e.g. in the early years a child may show an intense interest in Thomas the Tank Engine but later in childhood the interests might switch to Dr Who or types of weather). Some children may become preoccupied with a topic to such an extent that it interferes with academic life. They may lack the motivation to complete work which is unrelated to their special interest. Furthermore, the difficulties with social interaction which are characteristic of ASD will be exacerbated by these children's insistence on speaking about topics of particular interest to them. This can often lead to problems making and keeping friends and can leave them vulnerable to bullying.

Occasionally, a child's area of special interest may happen to be one which is also valued by peers and considered socially acceptable (e.g. football teams, computer games, horses or ballet). Whilst peers might initially be impressed by a child's detailed knowledge of such topics, however, they can quickly tire of hearing lists of facts and figures and of having their side of the conversation ignored! The child with ASD may therefore require explicit instruction and coaching in how to relinquish their turn in conversation and listen to the contributions of others.

Compulsions

Compulsions are behaviours which the child with ASD feels obliged to complete again and again to avoid unpleasant emotions, such as anxiety. Children with ASD will experience intense distress if their compulsive behaviour is interrupted and they do not get to complete it fully. This feature can pose a problem at school and may interfere with the learning of the child with ASD. On occasion, the child's compulsive behaviour can also interfere with the learning of classmates. First, the compulsion itself can cause disruption during class (e.g. the child who distracts others' attention due to a compulsion to empty the bins). Second, if an attempt is made to stop the child from completing the compulsive behaviour, the resultant anxiety can interfere with his/her learning (e.g. the child will be unable to process the teacher's directions due to intense distress and the continued urge to complete the behaviour in full). Over time, repeated instances can lead to the child falling behind with schoolwork. On occasion, attempts to interrupt the child's compulsive behaviour can lead to challenging outbursts which disrupt the learning of the whole class.

CAUTION

If teaching staff notice that a child is experiencing significant distress related to compulsive behaviour, it will be important for them to discuss this with the child's parents/carers and seek consent to obtain professional advice. If obsessive-compulsive disorder (OCD) is suspected by teachers or parents/carers, the child should be seen by a GP with a view to a possible referral to a child and adolescent psychiatrist or psychologist via the local Child and Adolescent Mental Health Service (CAMHS), if appropriate (see Chapter 10 for a description of OCD in the context of ASD).

Rituals and routines

Children with ASD often have a preference for sameness and therefore insist that they or others follow particular routines. They may become upset and anxious if these routines are disrupted (e.g. a change in the daily timetable to accommodate school assembly or being asked to change for PE before rather than after lunch). Such rituals and routines may make little sense to other people (e.g. the child who, upon arrival at school, neglects to respond to greetings from all of his peers until he has first lined up the pencils on his desk). The source of a child's distress at school may not be immediately obvious to school staff and may relate to a change of routine at home (e.g. a child may arrive tearful and angry due to a parent/carer taking a different route to school or having a different food than usual in a lunchbox). Good communication between home and school will help to ensure that everyone is aware of changes which might affect the child's behaviour.

 # HOW CAN WE HELP?

There are a number of ways in which teachers can help children with ASD to overcome the barriers to learning and social interaction which arise from their difficulties with imagination and flexibility of thought. Below are two advice sections, consisting of:

- **Proactive strategies:** This includes general strategies which, first, will help to create a predictable environment for the child and, second, help to manage transition during the school day.

- **Management strategies:** These are specific adaptations or activities aimed at capitalising on the child's strengths to promote learning and social interaction.

Proactive strategies: strategies aimed at creating predictability

Most children with ASD require predictability and are at their best when they know what to expect. When the environment is predictable and structured, children with ASD feel more secure and this enhances their independence. The provision of an appropriately structured school environment means that children with ASD will have less need to impose their own order and will present as less rigid in their behaviour. The following are some ways of maximising predictability at school and thus promoting learning for the child with ASD:

- **Using a timetable:** Provide children with a clear timetable for the school day or week that they can carry with them (children with ASD will benefit from a timetable with pictures if they have language difficulties, or one involving written words if they have good reading comprehension).

- **Sticking to the timetable:** Avoid unnecessary deviations from the child's routine as the child needs to be able to trust in any plan presented (e.g. the weekly timetable should reflect the plan as accurately as possible).

- **Preparing the child for changes to the environment:** Avoid changes to the physical environment, and be aware that when these are made they may be difficult for a child with

ASD to manage (e.g. let the class know in advance that you will be moving the posters in the classroom around and make sure that the child with ASD has understood this).

- **Preparing the child for changes to routine:** Prepare the child in advance by discussing changes to routine. It may be helpful to give the child a reason as to why the change is being made. Social Stories (see Appendix 8) can also be useful for teaching a child what to expect and how to cope with novel situations (e.g. you might write a Social Story to explain the expected behaviour on a school outing).

- **Dealing with unstructured periods:** Ensure that all parts of the day have sufficient structure and predictability. Check that the child is comfortable with what will happen during unstructured periods such as break and lunch time. If necessary, try to provide a comfortable activity during these times (see Chapter 6, Planning and Organisation Problems and Appendix 12 for the Lunch Time Activity Timetable).

- **Dealing with unexpected change:** Manage unexpected changes to routine by taking time to explain that there will be a deviation from the expected course of events. State clearly what the new plan is. If necessary, you might have to give the child a new timetable to reflect the change in routine or clearly mark the new plan on the existing one. Visual schedules and timetables (even ones drawn impromptu on a piece of paper!) can be incredibly powerful in reducing anxiety for the child with ASD (see Appendix 10 for Personalised Timetable and also Chapter 9, Challenging Behaviour).

- **Strategies aimed at managing transition during the school day:** Difficulties with change make times of transition at school difficult for many children with ASD. These transitions can go unnoticed by staff and other children, but feel like major events for a person with ASD, sometimes resulting in panic or tantrums. Behavioural difficulties of children with ASD can flare up at apparently minor transition points. A child with ASD may struggle when moving from one activity to another within a lesson, going from break back to class or vice versa, or starting and ending the school day. There are several things teachers can do to help children manage transition:

  - **Thinking ahead:** Be aware of when you are asking a child to make a transition, and anticipate potential difficulties (e.g. if you are aware that the child particularly enjoys the current activity, think through how you will handle the possible refusal to switch to doing something else).

  - **Counting down to transition:** Prepare the child for transition, telling them what will happen and when (e.g. let the child know they have 'three more minutes' or 'two more turns' to finish something). It may be helpful for children to have an unobtrusive digital clock or watch left on the desk so that they can keep track of time.

  - **Facilitating the transition:** If you suspect that the child does not know how to make the transition, be explicit about what they will need to do. Prompt cards can be helpful for this (see Chapter 6 and Appendix 11).

  - **Rewarding the child:** Use plenty of positive reinforcement when children behave appropriately during a transition. Over time they can build their capacity to manage change independently. Praising them for a good transition builds self-esteem and makes it more likely that the behaviour will be repeated next time.

Management strategies: strategies aimed at capitalising on the child's strengths

When an individual has a special interest or activity that they find very motivating, this can provide an opportunity to promote learning. The trick is to creatively harness the motivation to pursue a special interest in activities that foster development.

- **Using the special interest as a reward:** Allowing children to pursue their special interest can be a powerful reward for doing a less favoured activity (e.g. a child might be allowed time on the computer only after a maths exercise has been attempted).

- **Incorporating the interest into schoolwork:** Learning can be promoted through the child's pursuit of their area of special interest. A child obsessed with the London Underground could develop literacy skills by writing about some aspect of this transport system. A child who loves computers might learn to spell better using a computerised literacy programme. Someone with a strong interest in wildlife could build their communication skills by giving a talk on this topic.

- **Building self-esteem and confidence:** Self-esteem can also be built from special interests. Many children with ASD are at their highest functioning when working on something related to their area of special interest, and can earn praise this way from teachers and even peers (e.g. a child with an interest in maths might be supported in helping other children with their work, carefully overseen by the teacher).

- **Facilitating social interaction:**

    - **Making the interest 'social':** Unfortunately, all too often the topics which are of special interest to children with ASD are not those which are especially interesting to other children. Peers may initially be interested in joining in a conversation about cars, for example, until discovering that it is in fact tyre depth measurements which the child with ASD finds fascinating. It is important, therefore, to examine how the child's apparently solitary interest can be turned into a route to social interaction with peers. Think about creating a 'role' within the school for the child which will require other children to interact with him/her. For example, a child with an excellent memory for football scores might be put in charge of recording the score for school games. All class groups can be asked to report their scores to this child following matches.

    - **Training in social interaction:** As noted earlier, peers can quickly tire of discussing the special interests of the child with ASD if the conversation is one-sided and they don't get to take a turn. Children with ASD may therefore benefit from explicit instruction and coaching in how to relinquish their turn in the conversation and listen to the contributions of others. The use of resources such as turn-taking cards (Appendix 6), Social Stories (Appendix 8) or the use of the strategies described in Chapter 2 (Social Interaction) can be of help in teaching the child these skills.

■ **Using the interest to reduce anxiety:** A special interest can often be the main means of relaxation and source of enjoyment for the child with ASD. The area of interest can provide relief from certain intrusive thoughts or the stress of social interaction (e.g. half an hour working alone on a science project at lunch time may be an excellent way of relieving anxiety for a child with an interest in this area).

■ **Thinking about the future:** A special interest can, when creatively shaped and encouraged, form the basis for a future vocation (e.g. a child with an intense interest in computers could be encouraged to follow a career in IT). The child with ASD should be encouraged and helped to research possible careers which may utilise their great interest in particular topics.

 # FINAL CONSIDERATIONS

Although difficulties with imagination and flexible thinking can cause difficulties for the child with ASD they can also be considered positive attributes when channeled appropriately. With the right kind of organisation and support (e.g. providing predictability and structure throughout the school day), potential barriers to learning for children with ASD can be overcome, enabling them to realise their full academic potential. The special interests shown by some children with ASD can be viewed as a strength if used to promote learning, self-esteem and social acceptance. Creativity on the part of skilled education staff has turned many a solitary pursuit into one which gives children regular opportunities for social interaction.

CHAPTER 5

BULLYING

WHY IS THIS IMPORTANT?

The importance of addressing bullying has been widely recognised and addressed over the past ten years. Schools have widely implemented anti-bullying policies. Sadly, surveys show that pupils with special educational needs are one of the most vulnerable groups and children with ASD, who have both 'invisible' and primarily 'social disability,' are at a greater risk of being bullied. Statistics indicate that 75% of all children experience some form of bullying throughout their school years.

Although the prevalence rates of bullying being experienced by pupils with ASD vary, research indicates that children with ASD are four times more likely to be bullied than their non-disabled peers. As the transition to a new school is likely to be more difficult for pupils with ASD, specific and proactive focus on this issue has been reported to be one of the most helpful forms of support that a school can provide for pupils with ASD and one of the most appreciated by their parents.

WHAT DO WE NEED TO KNOW ABOUT BULLYING?

The consequences of bullying

- Bullying has a detrimental effect on the child's self-esteem, self-worth and academic achievement.

- Persistent bullying is often associated with mental health problems such as psychological distress, anxiety and depression, and can even lead to development of post-traumatic stress.

- Bullied children are six times more likely to contemplate suicide than their peers, and each year persistent bullying leads to 10–14 suicides amongst young people in the UK.[1]

- Bullying is one of the most frequent causes of school refusal and possibly placement breakdown, if the bullying is persistent.

Bullying and ASD

- As ASD is primarily a social disability, the children with ASD find it much harder to 'fit in' or may be perceived by their peers as 'uncool'.

- Their difficulty with making and sustaining friendships means that children with ASD are less likely to have a strong social network (see Chapter 2, Social Interaction).

- As children with ASD have difficulty with reading social cues, they often are very gullible, which makes them an 'easy target'.

- As ASD is an 'invisible' disability it is much more difficult for peers to understand the nature of the child's difficulties.

- Children with ASD can often display behaviours that upset their peers. For example, they may be very literal and say things that may offend other children – things that may be literally true (for example, that someone has a big spot on their face).

- ASD is often associated with unusual preoccupations, repetitive interests or sensory sensitivities, which can make children act in a way that is perceived as 'odd' by their peers, and hence present a 'perfect' opportunity for teasing or bullying.

- Children with ASD tend to have difficulties with social communication and may even misunderstand friendly joking as teasing or bullying.

- Bullies often have the social insight to time their bullying well (e.g. not to get caught by the teacher) and know the 'right buttons to press' to get a reaction. Children with ASD often do not have good coping skills and often end up getting into trouble whilst being 'caught' retaliating.

- Bullying is frequently under-reported for children who have significant difficulty with verbal and nonverbal communication of their emotions.

Challenges for teachers

Whilst most teachers are well aware of the specific vulnerabilities of children with ASD listed above, tackling them is a very complex task and requires skilled, creative and individualised support. This can be particularly challenging given the competing demands of managing a busy classroom, meeting curriculum requirements and managing the often contrasting needs of a wide

---

1   As a result, authors Neil Marr and Tim Field wrote a book entitled 'Bullycide: Death at Playtime', documenting cases of children's suicides related to persistent and severe bullying in the UK (Marr & Field, 2001).

range of pupils. The examples below illustrate some of the most frequent and disempowering issues teachers reported:

- 'We are all aware that isolated pupils are at greatest risk of being bullied, but how can we make other children like them and be friends with them?'

- 'The problem is that they do these things/act in such ways that they invite negative reactions from their peer group all the time'

- 'If our teachers adopt a different set of rules for them, it will make them look different and we are worried it will increase their social isolation'

- 'The child comes to our office every day and reports being bullied. But I was there for the latest incident and saw what happened. A child literally just ran past and bumped into her, by accident, but she felt she was being targeted on purpose. How do I distinguish which incidents are really serious and which were just innocent friendly jokes or approaches made by other children?'

This list is not exhaustive; it is just an example of the most common dilemmas as well as some of the trickiest issues teachers shared with us. As every school and every pupil is different, a successful approach requires personalisation of the suggested strategies. Given below is a summary of a wide range of strategies created by teachers, SENCOs, anti-bullying charities, researchers, psychologists and people with ASD themselves, who dedicate their time and effort into supporting children with ASD who experience bullying.

 HOW CAN WE HELP?

There are several ways of approaching the pervasive problem of bullying. The government guidelines emphasise three key areas: the importance of acknowledging bullying, preventing bullying, and involving the whole school and wider community to establish clear management procedures to tackle bullying. Below are two advice sections, consisting of:

- **Proactive strategies:** This section highlights the importance of increasing the awareness of bullying as a first step towards addressing the problem. The overall aim is to increase the students' ability to report instances of bullying and for teachers to identify those who are vulnerable and recognise situations related to bullying issues. This will enable schools to implement and monitor adherence to their anti-bullying policies.

- **Management strategies:** This section reviews important strategies to deal with the bully and support the victim of the bullying (see Appendix 18).

Proactive strategies: increasing awareness

- **Empowering teachers**

  - **School climate and anti-bullying policy:** As emphasised by the government guidelines, the 'whole school approach' has been found to be the most effective anti-bullying policy by far. However, implementing the guidelines can be a challenge, given the many specific needs and challenges pupils with ASD may have. Factors which can really make a difference are the creation of the appropriate school climate, a clear, regularly reviewed and updated anti-bullying policy and a sustained focus on the issue over time.

  - **Psycho-education:** In order to prevent bullying, effective measures must be implemented to cover all areas related to the school day. This includes playground or lunch times, during which pupils with ASD can be most vulnerable. These times can be difficult as the teachers who know the child with ASD best may not be available to provide supervision. It is suggested that distributing the Pupil Profile to all school staff is an invaluable measure designed to ensure the specific needs and idiosyncratic behaviours of children with ASD are thoroughly understood.

  - **Support:** Reporting incidents of bullying can be difficult for teachers as well as those being bullied. Teachers may be concerned that it might raise parent/carer anxiety, or shed a negative light on the school. Or they might be concerned about how it will be perceived, for example, that they might have difficulty managing the needs of the particular pupil. It is important to recognise and reiterate to all staff that preventing bullying, especially where pupils with ASD are concerned, can be a very challenging task. Teachers should be encouraged to seek support from the whole staff team. Placing importance on investigating the concerns of staff should be at the centre of any approach, regardless of how minor the incidents may be.

- **Empowering pupils with ASD**

  - **Recognising bullying:** Difficulties with social insight associated with ASD mean that pupils with this condition can be extremely socially naïve. It is not uncommon for pupils with ASD to misinterpret the intentions of others. Pupils with ASD are often so keen to form friendships that they may not recognise when they are being 'used' to do inappropriate things in exchange for the seemingly 'friendly' behaviours of others. They are vulnerable to being manipulated in order to gain the acceptance of the peer group (see Chapter 2, Social Interaction). Pupils with ASD can therefore strongly benefit from clear explanations of what constitutes different types of bullying (including cyberbullying) or unacceptable behaviour. This may need to be outlined as one of the targets in their Transition Management Plan and worked through during specific one-to-one times, or during PHSE lessons. However, if this issue is being tackled with the whole class, it is important to be mindful that pupils with ASD may need a lot more specific input around this issue than most of their peers.

- **Reporting of bullying:** Difficulties with communication associated with ASD can result in pupils having significant difficulty reporting incidents of bullying. Even pupils with excellent language abilities may struggle in describing complex social situations. In contrast to their good understanding of other more factual information, they may not fully comprehend the subtleties of such situations (see Chapter 3, Difficulties). Having access to a regular, confidential and safe space with a trusted member of staff, even if it is only for 15 minutes per week, can be invaluable in helping pupils with ASD to talk through their concerns.

- **Dealing with helplessness:** It is important to recognise that many pupils with ASD will arrive at secondary school with a long history of bullying in their primary school or other settings. Thus, many pupils may have acquired a so-called 'learned helplessness' and think that nothing can be done about the situation anyway. Many pupils therefore may not report incidents of bullying for fear that it would not change things, or that it would make things worse. As a result, children with ASD may not use the confidential bully-boxes that some schools use, and instead may need a proactive approach from a trusted member of staff to help them to open up about their experiences, and a reassurance that their concerns will be taken seriously and properly addressed.

- **Psycho-education about the impact of behaviour:** Children with ASD may often have specific behaviours which make them appear 'different' and thus more obvious targets for bullies. Whilst children with ASD can work on developing more prosocial or adaptive ways of behaving, it is important in the first instance to carefully consider which aspects of behaviour can realistically be addressed by the pupil, and which cannot reasonably be expected to change. For example, if a pupil feels the compulsion to perform certain specific rituals, ways can be found of teaching them to enact these in a safe and private space, if possible. However, if the pupil needs to wear ear defenders, for example, to help them with their sensory sensitivities, this is not a behaviour that the child may be able to alter and it could make them stand out from their peers. It is therefore very important to ensure that the pupil with ASD is not being discriminated against on the grounds of their disability. However, if there are behaviours which can be worked on or altered, it may prove useful to have a specific plan aimed at helping the child tackle these. For example, this can be done either directly, through a social skills group in which more prosocial behaviours can be taught, or during one-to-one sessions, using pictures or Social Stories (see Appendix 8). Alternatively, these can be managed environmentally, by allocating certain times and safe places where the pupil can engage in private in the behaviours associated with their condition.

- **Identifying vulnerable times:** This can be a very effective strategy for preventing bullying in situations when other strategies have proven difficult to apply. Pupils with ASD are particularly vulnerable during unstructured times, such as breaks, lunch times or playground activities. The reasons for this are three-fold. First, because children with ASD find unstructured times the most difficult, this can often result in increased anxiety and consequently engagement in repetitive behaviour or other kinds of noticeable behaviour, which may attract bullying. Second, children with ASD do not tend to have as good a social network as other children, and the possible ensuing isolation is one of the highest risk factors for bullying. Third, the risk of bullying may be increased during unstructured times when the same level of adult supervision is unavailable. If certain times present a particular risk, it would be beneficial to help the pupil by structuring proactive activities, such as engagement in lunch-time clubs, if possible, or in other planned constructive activities with peers.

- **Awareness of pupil's vulnerabilities during lessons:** Certain lessons may pose higher risk for covert or less obvious bullying than others. For example, PE can be particularly challenging, as most pupils with ASD have difficulty with motor coordination and therefore never get picked for teams or are always the last ones chosen. However, other lessons where group work is encouraged may also pose similar risks as children with ASD may not have many friends. If this is a risk, teachers may need to be advised to take a more active role in structuring the groups and allocating the pupil with ASD to work with children with higher social sensitivity, who will be more likely to include them.

- **Encouraging social integration and social network:** Pupils with ASD struggle to make friends, although they often have invaluable qualities to offer to others, such as loyalty, reliability, trustworthiness, and specific skills or knowledge. Helping to create opportunities for peers to discover the qualities of a child with ASD can facilitate the development of peer-bonding and strengthen the social network for the child with ASD. This can be achieved by focusing on group dynamics, individual characteristics of children, and meaningful connections which could be formed. For example, the child with ASD who excels in academic work can be paired up with a socially sensitive and skilled child who struggles academically, so both can support each other in reciprocal ways.

- **Supporting the peers**

  - **Awareness of the power of 'bystanders':** Bullying can occur only if there is an imbalance of power. The more support from others the bully has, the more power imbalance s/he has achieved. If the bully has no support from others, their attempts to bully will be futile, socially challenged and rejected, and consequently unlikely to occur again, as support from peers would give the victim more 'power' than the bully. All children therefore need to be made aware of their own power as bystanders, and their responsibility in supporting bullying. Although many children have this awareness, they may be afraid of standing up for the victim, for fear of making themselves the victim next time. All children need to be confident that they will not be the only ones standing up for the victim, but that they will also be supported by their peers. This can be achieved by a particular focus on this issue within the PHSE lessons, or, for example, during the 'Circle of Friends' time (see Appendix 9).

  - **Encouraging of reporting:** If children do not feel that they are able to intervene during the incidents of bullying, it is important to think of a way to encourage them at least to report it confidentially. Children may need continuous reminders and encouragement to do so, as well as reassurance, in order to find courage and feel a collective responsibility for a more vulnerable member of the group.

- **Awareness of the pupil's difficulties:** ASD is an 'invisible disability'. Whilst bullying of a child with a clearly recognised disability would be a lot more likely to be socially and morally unacceptable and judged, many children may not understand why a child with ASD may sometimes behave in unusual ways. Hence, peers may be a lot less likely to stand up for a child with ASD as compared to a child with other disabilities. The best solution would be to discuss the diagnosis and its impact with the child's peers, as long as the child and parents/carers consent to it. In general, talking about a wide range of difficulties, for example during the PHSE lessons, would be helpful. Implementing a programme that encourages learning in an experiential rather than theoretical way is likely to be most effective.

- **Facilitating a social support network:** Helping the child with ASD to develop a positive support network and genuine friendships can significantly contribute to reducing the risk of them being bullied, in addition to other benefits (see Chapter 2, Social Interaction).

- **Reinforcing positive examples of behaviour:** During tutorials, mentoring groups and whole-school assemblies, positive examples of pupils' behaviour towards each other can be highlighted in order to reinforce kind, considerate, prosocial behaviour in school.

Management strategies: strategies for dealing with bullying

- **Understanding and reporting the incident**

  - **Understanding the incident:** Ensure that all members of staff are aware of the child's difficulties with communication, which tend to worsen with increased anxiety. A child with ASD is often not socially skilled, and is therefore often the one to get 'caught' when they try to defend themselves. It is therefore important to allow the child with ASD to calm down and give them support and more time to explain what has happened in order to understand the incident from both sides.

  - **Recording the incidents:** All incidents of bullying need to be recorded, in line with the school's policy. To help monitor these incidents it would be helpful to devise a way of recording the place and time they take place so that potential patterns can be identified. This can help to ensure the safety of potential victims of bullying.

- **Dealing with perpetrators of bullying**

  - **Sanctions:** Consequences of potential future incidents of bullying need to be made very clear, as well as rewards for peers who supported the victim or reported any incidents. Consistency in carrying out the sanctions is the key.

  - **Facilitating understanding in bullies:** If bullies are aware of the victim's disability, explain to them how ASD impacts on the victim's behaviour and that bullying of anyone, particularly a person with disability, is highly unacceptable. If the family or the child did not consent to their diagnosis being discussed with peers, a more general discussion about specific difficulties we all have can be held instead. However, it is important to ensure that bullies do not use this discussion as further 'ammunition' for future bullying, clearly stating consequences of such behaviour.

- **Treating all incidents as serious:** If the bullies try to belittle the incident by stating they were just joking, it needs to be explained (if they are aware of the child's diagnosis) that the victim may have difficulties with understanding certain jokes. If bullies are not aware of the victim's disability, they may need an alternative explanation of why such jokes are not acceptable and will not be tolerated in the future.

- **Making amends:** It is important for the bullies to apologise to the victim, and for this apology to be supervised, to ensure it is not offered in a 'mocking', but a genuine style.

- **Facilitating positive behaviour in bullies:** Incidents of bullying can also occur when potential bullies may not have other, more constructive activities to engage in. Perpetrators of bullying can be helped to find positive activities to occupy them. However, it is important to ensure that this is not perceived as a 'reward' by the victim or other children and that it is understood and applied only as a way of helping the child who is acting as a bully whom, it must be acknowledged, also has difficulties albeit in a different area.

- **Supporting victims of bullying**

  - **Reassurance:** The child with ASD will need reinforcement to build their confidence and courage to report any incidents of bullying. The child will greatly benefit from reassurance that these will be taken seriously.

  - **Victim safety:** Ensuring the safety of the victim is paramount. Allocating a safe place for the child to go to when they are feeling anxious, ensuring that all staff members are aware that the child is allowed to use such a safe place when they need to and scheduling proactive times for the pupil to discuss their concerns with a trusted adult can all be invaluable in achieving victim safety.

  - **Teaching responses to incidents of bullying:** Children with ASD often tend to have difficulties with regulating their emotions. When anxious, children with ASD are vulnerable to having 'meltdowns'. These can further empower bullies, as they have achieved a goal of getting a reaction from the child with ASD. Alternatively, children with ASD can respond with challenging behaviour when they are not able to defend themselves verbally. Pupils can be taught helpful responses to attempted bullying through Social Stories or pictures, or by using lists of strategies. Children with ASD may need concrete instructions on what is and what is not an acceptable response to bullying. Pupils should be taught not only what not to do, but also an alternative of what to do instead. These can include instructions on where to go for safety or who ask for help, or learning specific 'comebacks' which can be applicable across a range of situations, such as saying 'whatever' and walking away.

  - **Relaxation techniques:** Pupils with a long-standing history of being bullied can develop enhanced sensitivity and increased levels of anxiety. Simple relaxation techniques can help with ameliorating the negative impact of persistent bullying on a pupil's mental wellbeing, providing that victim safety has been ensured (see Appendix 22).

- **Enhancing social support network:** Social isolation is one of the highest risk factors, which makes children with ASD an 'easy target' for bullying. Discussing bullying during such activities as the 'Circle of Friends' time can be an extremely helpful strategy for empowering other children to take turns in supporting the pupil and to ensure they are not left alone during the most vulnerable times, such as breaks. This discussion can provide a helpful opportunity for peers to come up with their own creative ideas of how to support the child with ASD. It can also increase children's confidence in standing up to bullies, knowing that other members of the Circle of Friends will support them (see Appendices 9 and 18). A pupil with ASD can in turn offer them help with particular aspects of homework or subjects they might be good at (such as IT or history), or any other area of strength.

CAUTION

What to do if problems with bullying persist despite best efforts

Bullying can be the most persistent and troubling problem throughout the early lives of children with ASD. In these cases, more targeted and intensive support may be needed. Common scenarios which can prove particularly problematic are where the child with ASD repeatedly misinterprets unintentional events as incidents of bullying and where a child with ASD is perceived as bullying others. Sensitive, skilled handling by schools can help to diffuse and manage these situations effectively so that the problems do not recur. Teachers and parents/ carers should consult Appendix 18 for advice regarding management of such issues. The 'Helpful resources' section of Appendix 18 lists organisations which can be contacted for further advice and support. A referral to the local Child and Adolescent Mental Health Service (CAMHS) should always be sought in situations linked to bullying where staff have concerns about the mental health of any child.

FINAL CONSIDERATIONS

Sadly, combating bullying is not a straightforward process. However, it can be one of the most satisfying aspects of working with children in a school environment. Witnessing how much children for whom this issue has been a persistent problem can blossom with support, as well as the gratitude from their parents/carers, will make every step of the process more than worthwhile and memorable. Whilst the strategies outlined here were designed for children with ASD, many other children can benefit from these techniques also. Government guidelines emphasise that a continuous focus on the overall issue of preventing bullying is the key, rather than amelioration of the secondary issues, which can often be a lot more time consuming and, sadly, less rewarding to address.

CHAPTER 6

PLANNING AND ORGANISATION PROBLEMS

WHY IS THIS IMPORTANT?

Throughout childhood and adolescence, as the brain continues to develop, we acquire the ability to plan and organise our behaviour to work towards increasingly complex goals. At the age of 12, a child might be expected to pack their gym kit in the evening ready for school the next day. By the age of 20 the same person can generate and carry out complex plans to achieve a goal months or even years into the future, like arranging a summer holiday or moving to a new city.

The capacity for planning and organising is essential for living an independent and successful life.

Most people with an ASD struggle with planning and organising their own behaviour. This can seriously affect their ability to function and thrive at school. Some of the aspects of daily life that are significantly affected by planning and organisation problems are unstructured times or break times, homework and even the child's behaviour. Difficulties with planning and organising can have a significant effect on a child's ability to reach their full academic potential.

WHAT DO WE NEED TO KNOW ABOUT PLANNING AND ORGANISATION PROBLEMS?

Good planning and organisation skills are essential to prepare us for situations and enable us to achieve our goals. What will follow is a guide to:

- Identifying different types of skills involved in successful planning in order to be able to tailor specific strategies.

- Understanding the effect of planning and organisation problems in the school environment.

Identifying skills involved in successful planning and organisation

Many children with planning and organisational difficulties are misunderstood. Their inability to function in a classroom can be seen as a sign of laziness, naughtiness or a lack of understanding. These sorts of misunderstandings can be unhelpful for the child, and for those people trying to help them to perform better. Therefore it is really important to identify the underlying skills that can be affected (please view Appendix 23 for further examples of the ways in which difficulties with executive function can present themselves in daily life):

- **Goal setting:** A specific skill necessary for identifying or setting appropriate goals. This means that the pupil may have problems understanding how to approach complex open-ended tasks (e.g. coursework).

- **Planning:** The ability to develop a plan in order to work towards a goal. A child may start a project without a plan and may not know what to do next.

- **Prioritising:** The capacity needed to appropriately allocate time to tasks according to their importance. Children with difficulty in this area may spend all their time on one small part of an overall task. They may also struggle with tasks such as note-taking.

- **Organising:** The ability to manage the materials needed to work towards goals. The pupil may arrive at lessons without the necessary materials.

- **Initiating:** The skills required to independently start a given task. Children with difficulties in this area often become 'stuck' from the outset as they do not know how and where to begin.

- **Short-term memory:** The capability of a child to hold a certain amount of information in their mind whilst processing it (e.g. remembering instructions with several steps). Pupils with this difficulty may appear to be inattentive, but have actually forgotten what they are supposed to do owing to their memory difficulties.

- **Flexibility:** The capacity to move flexibly from one activity or train of thought to another when working towards a goal. Pupils with this difficulty may struggle with transitions during the day. Often they persist with an approach to a task even when it is not working or do not seem to be able to shift from one aspect of a task to another.

- **Monitoring:** The ability of a child to keep track of their own performance and compare their output to their goal and plan. A child with this difficulty may not check or notice their mistakes.

- **Generalising:** The ability to transfer and apply a skill learned in one environment to another. Difficulties with generalisation are a well-recognised problem area for children with ASD. Whilst they frequently excel in rote learning, children with ASD are often at a total loss as to how and when to apply their learned skills in different settings.

Understanding the effects of planning and organisation problems in a school environment

If a child has significant difficulties with planning and organisation this will have an impact on their ability to function and perform well at school in a number of ways. In order to help them, it will be important to think about how planning and organisation difficulties are having an impact on them, which will enable us to anticipate when and with which activities the child is likely to need support.

In general, the following situations during structured and unstructured times can pose a challenge to children with planning and organisation difficulties:

- **Structured classroom times**

  - **Coursework:** Can be especially demanding in terms of planning and organisation, as the child is required to work towards a goal at some time in the future, the achievement of which requires generating and following through a complex plan.

  - **Managing materials:** Presents a challenge for many children, and it is especially hard for those with planning and organisational problems. In particular, 'remembering to remember' can be particularly difficult, and so materials are often forgotten or lost. Consequently, the child may appear to be unmotivated or disinterested in the session, having failed to prepare the necessary materials or bring appropriate clothing (e.g. PE kit).

  - **Practical sessions:** Such as science experiments or design and technology classes, often require children to plan independently and execute complex sequences of behaviour, and can be challenging for children with planning and organisation problems. At times when they are struggling they may become disengaged from the lesson, or may misbehave as a way of expressing their frustration or relieving their boredom.

  - **Test and exam performance:** Requires a range of planning and organisational skills, such as time management, prioritising tasks and planning answers. These are particularly difficult to execute when anxiety is high, and children with planning and organisational problems are likely to struggle when being formally evaluated. As a result, these children often significantly underachieve during exams, despite thorough preparation.

- **Unstructured times**

  - **Homework:** Is a struggle for many children, but those with planning and organisational problems have particular difficulties in this area even when they are motivated to perform the work. Successfully completing and handing in homework relies upon a range of abilities, including noting down the assignment, remembering it, managing time and organising materials. Furthermore, all planning and organisational skills as described above (e.g. goal setting, planning, initiating and monitoring) are required to complete homework successfully. As this tends to be a significant problem for most children with ASD, please see Appendix 20 for further information and helpful management strategies.

  - **Unsupervised leisure time:** Brings with it social challenges, and is often difficult to manage for children with ASD. It is even harder for those with additional planning and organisational problems, because children often end up feeling at a loss without an external structure being provided for them. Children with planning and organisational problems may struggle to work out what to do at break times, or who to join. As a result, they are more likely to become anxious at these times, during which they can also be particularly vulnerable (e.g. feel lonely or be at risk of being bullied).

- **Transitions:** Are especially difficult for children with ASD, both due to the difficulty with flexibility that is characteristic of ASD and the problems they have anticipating what will happen and what is expected of them. Transitions include the start and end of the school day, moving between lessons (especially when this involves moving location), the start and end of breaks and even shifting activities within a lesson. For these children, transitions can be very stressful. They may resist change and display inappropriate behaviour because of their anxiety or frustration (see Chapter 8, Anxiety).

- **Unsupervised work:** Can present a challenge for children with planning and organisation problems because it requires them to set goals and then work towards these without external support from a teacher (e.g. independent classroom assignments or projects). In these situations they may become confused, fail to attempt the correct task or lose sight of their goals and of how to achieve these.

- **Generalisation:** Tends to be an area of significant difficulty for all children with ASD to varying degrees. Pupils with ASD tend to be predominantly concrete thinkers and may take instructions quite literally. This means that although they may have learnt a skill easily, they may not be able to recognise when it can be applied in different settings. As a result they may rely more on specific prompts from a teacher for things that are implicit and do not need to be made obvious to most other students.

 ## HOW CAN WE HELP?

It is worth remembering that we all use strategies to improve our planning and organisation (e.g. writing a 'to do' list at the start of a busy week, keeping an appointments diary, making sure we always leave our wallet and keys in the same place so that we can find them in the morning). These are examples of strategies we use to help us to deal with the various complex organisational challenges of our lives.

Two sections below detail strategies to support children with planning and organisation problems:

- **Proactive strategies:** for organisation and planning

- **Management strategies:** for organisation and planning.

Proactive strategies for organisation and planning

- **Try not to overload the child**

  Focus on prioritising the most important instructions, simplifying the demands and clarifying the expectations. The more complex the task, the higher the risk of confusion and demoralisation. Being aware of the child's processing speed and delivering new information at their pace will increase their ability to fully understand instructions.

- **Organising materials**

  This is one of the most common difficulties for children with ASD. The following strategies can be useful in helping children organise themselves better:

  - **Use of checklists to help remember items:** Having checklists (for example, attaching the list of materials needed each day to the timetable) is very helpful for children with organisation problems. At first the child will not be able to make use of these lists independently, as they will forget to look at them. Parents/carers and teachers will have to prompt the child to consult and use the lists at appropriate times. After a while, adults should try to draw back their support in this area, once the child has established the habit of using the lists.

  - **Advance planning:** Support children with particular difficulties with organisation by taking a couple of minutes before the lesson begins to prepare all their materials. It is recommended that it is explicitly explained to the child that even though they may lose a few minutes of their break time, it may help prevent them from falling behind their peers from the start of the lesson. Pre-planning may also help to reduce the stress caused by the child being unable to find the right materials whilst the teacher is already giving instructions to the class. It might also be helpful for teachers to provide the student with a written sequence of the required tasks.

  - **Colour coding:** Using colour-coded timetables with a corresponding colour for the materials for each subject can help the child remember to find and bring the right materials to the class (e.g. using the colour red for maths on the timetable as well as a red maths folder or a red cover on the maths book). This is particularly helpful for children who have difficulties with locating their things (e.g. in their school bag) and also children who tend to become anxious or stressed if they cannot find something immediately.

- **Managing transitions with prompt cards and timetables**

  Children who experience difficulty with flexibility, anticipating and understanding changes are likely to benefit from the following types of help:

  - **Consistent use of a timetable to establish a predictable routine:** At first, the child is likely to need regular prompts to consult the timetable until they become familiar with the day's structure and can remember to use it independently (see Appendix 10, Personalised Timetable). Predictability is very important for children with ASD, not only in terms of helping children with planning and organisation, but also in helping to reduce anxiety. For pupils who tend to feel particularly anxious during the unstructured times, a special timetable could be drawn up (see Appendix 12 as an example of a lunch time activity timetable).

- **Advance prompts to remind the child about upcoming transitions:** Teachers can prepare the child for upcoming changes and transitions by giving a verbal prompt to the whole class (or just the child) by reminding them of the remaining time available (e.g. a two-minute warning that the lesson is about to end).

- **Preparing the child for a change:** Changes tend to be particularly difficult for pupils with ASD. They present increased demands on flexibility, planning and understanding of the expectations of their environment, all of which can be a challenge. Children with ASD benefit from being prepared for any change to their regular routine as soon as possible (e.g. preparing a child for a field trip or a sports day, and outlining what will happen).

- **Supporting memory**
Children experiencing difficulty with so-called 'working' memory tend to struggle with following instructions and processing information. This can often cause academic underachievement as well as frustration during lessons. The following strategies are recommended:

  - **Shorten the complexity of the instructions:** If possible, try to break down instructions into smaller chunks and present them one step at a time.

  - **Repeat new information or instructions:** If necessary, repeat new information for the child (or the whole class) and encourage the child to write down each step in their exercise book.

  - **Use visual instructions or step-by-step guides:** Providing prompt cards for the pupil outlining the different steps needed to complete more complex tasks can facilitate their ability to work independently. A similar approach can be used when presenting new information in order to enable the child to process it appropriately.

  - **Establish routines that place fewer burdens on memory:** Encourage the development of good habits, which may require reminders initially, but will become automatic after a certain period of time (e.g. a child, or the whole class, may be encouraged to lay out all the materials they will need at the beginning of a lesson before the work begins or to put homework in a tray before the first class of the day).

- **Facilitating generalisation**
When teaching a new skill, provide many different examples of when it can be applied. Encouraging the child to utilise this skill in different settings and environments will aid internalisation of the new information and a child's ability to generalise it.

- **Considering uneven learning profiles**
Children with ASD are known to often have unusually uneven cognitive profiles. The abilities of most typically developing children tend to be quite balanced, so that it is easy to estimate the range of their abilities. However, children with ASD often require an individually tailored curriculum according to their discrepant profile of strengths and difficulties. It is important to be mindful of these possible discrepancies in a pupil's learning profile. Children with

varying skills and strengths in some areas can appear uncooperative, defiant or not to be trying hard enough when they face an activity in which they have a significant weakness (e.g. a child whose vocabulary is years ahead of their peers can be at a total loss as to how to write an essay).

■ **Rewarding the process as well as the outcome**
Praise the child for attempting to set goals and make plans, not just for the successful completion of a task. Rewards are important in encouraging planning and organisation, as many of the strategies are quite boring for the child and do not carry inherent rewards.

Management strategies for organisation and planning

■ **Goal, Plan, Do, Review approach**

   ■ **Goal**
   When starting a task the child first needs to be clear about what their goal is. Once the child has been helped to work this out, it should be recorded on paper. Ideally this will mean that the child writes down the goal on their Goal, Plan, Do, Review worksheet (Appendix 19). Depending on the child's verbal abilities, it may be helpful to use a visual prompt such as a picture or symbol.

   ■ **Plan**
   Once the goal has been established the child needs to be encouraged to generate a plan. Children with ASD may struggle with generating ideas for an open-ended task. They often benefit from visual support to help them generate ideas and make links between these ideas. It is recommended that children are helped to use visual mind mapping. Planning can be a daunting task, but it can be made less so by breaking the planning process into steps, using a detailed outline. The BAT procedure can provide a helpful format for this:

      ■ Break down the task into bits during a brainstorming session, with the results recorded on paper, for example with a mind map.

      ■ Arrange the parts of the task sequentially, also on paper.

      ■ Timings can also be added into this plan.

   ■ **Do**
   The BAT plan they have generated should guide the child through the activity, but, depending on the severity of their particular planning and organisation problems, they may need support getting started, staying on track or shifting from one part of the checklist to the next. If this is the case, this should be done by referring the child back to the BAT plan. Stages on the plan should be ticked off as soon as they are accomplished to help the child keep track of where they are and to provide a sense of achievement.

   ■ **Review**
   Many children with planning and organisation problems do not spontaneously evaluate their own work. Once the BAT plan has been carried out, the child should be encouraged to review their work in relation to the plan and to their stated goal.

FINAL CONSIDERATIONS

Initially, helping children with planning and organisation difficulties involves providing support strategies externally to help guide their behaviour. However, over time and with practice, these external controls will be internalised by the child. By being guided through the process of planning and organising they will acquire the ability to do this increasingly independently. As the child develops a greater capacity for independent goal-directed behaviour, they will need less and less external support.

Thus the process involves gradually reducing the level of support a child receives, in line with their developing planning and organisation abilities. To facilitate the process of internalisation, be explicit with the child that they are learning strategies to help them with planning and organisation, and explain to them why this is important in order to motivate them. Finally, remember that practice makes perfect. Repeated and consistent support in the application of strategies is the key to success. Through repeating an identical strategy time and time again, children can internalise it and make it their own.

CHAPTER 7

SENSORY SENSITIVITIES

 WHY IS THIS IMPORTANT?

There is increasing evidence that sensory sensitivities are a significant issue for a substantial proportion of children with ASD. Sensory sensitivities include problems involving visual stimuli, noise and sound, taste, smell and touch. Whilst not all children with ASD are affected by sensory issues, for those who are, it can be one of their primary difficulties and sources of distress. As this is not something that children can learn to control, ensuring proactive support is paramount.

Sensory sensitivities can have a significant impact on children's concentration and ability to process stimuli around them, and consequently affect their behaviour. Children may feel overwhelmed by their environment and become withdrawn as they go into sensory overload. Children with ASD experience their environment differently and this can result in certain sensory stimuli being very unpleasant for them or even painful. For example, children with sensitivity to sounds may feel fear and anxiety when the bell rings at school.

Sensory sensitivities can also have secondary consequences. For example, they can result in bullying in response to the child's unusual reaction (e.g. child covering ears at noises they find unpleasant). It is important to identify whether the young person has sensory difficulties and exactly what these are.

 WHAT DO WE NEED TO KNOW ABOUT SENSORY ISSUES?

There are different types of sensory sensitivities (sometimes called 'sensory issues') as well as different reactions to them.

Types of sensory sensitivities

■ **Visual:** The child may be sensitive to light coming in through the windows or to artificial light in the classroom.

- **Noise and sounds:** The child may be sensitive to loud noises, like bells going off, or to the noises which naturally occur in gyms or dining halls.

- **Smell:** The child may be sensitive to smell or may even find some smells unpleasant, such as glues or paints found in art classes or smells from cookery classes or dining halls.

- **Touch and feel:** The child may be sensitive to the feel of their uniform or the labels inside the uniform. The child may not like to be touched by other children or conversely may like this sensation and seek to touch others.

Responses to sensitivities

Children with ASD may have different kinds of sensory issues:

- **Sensory hyper-sensitivity:** Is a significantly increased sensitivity to a particular sensory stimulus which can result in a child becoming overwhelmed, distressed or uncomfortable. Some sensory stimuli can be so distressing for the child that they become almost painful. Examples of hyper-sensitivity are:

  - Becoming distressed by volume or pitch of sounds

  - Being distracted by visual information/patterns/movements

  - Finding touch, some textures and changes in temperature uncomfortable/painful

  - Finding some smells overpowering, no matter how mild they seem to others.

- **Sensory hypo-sensitivity:** In contrast to being overly sensitive, some children with ASD may have a much reduced sensitivity to sensory stimuli than expected. Some children with ASD also have specific sensory fascinations (so-called sensory interests) and may actively seek out these stimuli, such as light patterns. Examples of hypo-sensitivity or sensory interests are:

  - Looking intensely at lights/patterns/objects

  - Putting their ears up close to the source of sounds

  - Not obviously reacting to pain/injuries

  - Enjoying strong tastes (of both edible and non-edible items).

CAUTION

Difficulties with identifying sensory issues

Sensory sensitivities can sometimes be difficult to identify because they may not be immediately apparent. Teachers may observe behaviours which initially may not seem to be linked to sensory sensitivities, and which can easily be perceived as unusual or attention-seeking (e.g. a child anxious about strong light or loud noises may refuse to enter a room 'for no apparent reason'). Challenging behaviour can also be a manifestation of a strong sensory issue. Identifying potential sensory issues through the Screening Questionnaires and during the Bridge Meeting can be effective in anticipating and proactively resolving potential problems.

HOW CAN WE HELP?

Because the processing of sensory stimuli in the brain is not within the child's voluntary control, the strategies outlined below will focus on supporting children through environmental adaptations:

- **Proactive strategies:** forward planning

- **Management strategies:** environmental adaptations.

Proactive strategies: forward planning

Once a child's potential sensory sensitivities have been identified, it is helpful to assess how these will affect the child in the new school environment. This is important in order to identify which level of management strategies will be necessary and effective for the child. Whilst some interventions can be very easy to implement (e.g. by changing the seating arrangements), others may require more planning (e.g. by finding an alternative environment), thus ascertaining the severity of the sensory issue is a beneficial first step. The following strategies may be useful in forward planning:

- Provide access to school buildings before transitioning to the new school, first when the school is empty and later with students and staff present. This allows the child to experience how their sensory sensitivities will affect them in the new school.

- Allow the child to become aware of the smells, lights and sounds that may be a characteristic of the new school. Depending on their sensitivity, it is crucial to ascertain which adaptations are necessary.

- If the child appears to have difficulty with a particular sensation, identify suitable management strategies based on other previously effective approaches deployed by the primary school or parents/carers, or on the basis of the suggestions below.

Management strategies: environmental adaptations

The following strategies have been found effective in minimising the impact of the child's sensory sensitivities on their academic performance, behaviour and wellbeing. What follows is a list of environmental adaptations for each sensory modality that teachers can employ depending on the level of the child's support needs. The feasibility of their application may vary from school to school. However, it is hoped that the broad range of suggestions below will enable schools to identify possible modifications and create an optimal environment for the child with the resources available.

- **Visual sensory issues**

    - Minimising the amount of visual distractions can be very effective in helping children to focus on the task at hand. An uncluttered classroom can reduce distraction for some children with ASD.

    - Allowing a child with light sensitivities to sit further away from the window if they find this unpleasant. This measure can enhance their concentration.

    - Checking fluorescent lights regularly and changing them when necessery will help reduce flickering (and humming) which can be highly distracting.

    - Using blinds to reduce glare and reflections (be mindful that blinds don't create distracting patterns or noise).

    - Giving the child the opportunity to work at a designated at work area can be a solution for children who are easily distracted.

- **Noise and sounds**

    - Minimising the amount of auditory distractions in a classroom can help (e.g. turning off electrical equipment when not in use helps to keep classroom noise to a minimum).

    - Providing a set place on the edge of the room away from noise or allowing the child to have access to an agreed quiet area can help in especially noisy areas such as dining rooms and sports halls.

    - Allowing the child to wear headphones or earplugs can limit distress caused by noises they find unpleasant.

    - Warning a child with ASD in advance of loud noises can be helpful too, especially if this is unavoidable (e.g. fire alarm tests or bells ringing to signal the end of a lesson).

    - Transitioning between classrooms in noisy corridors can be difficult for children with ASD with sensory sensitivities, so consider letting the child leave the class earlier, when it is quieter.

    - Reducing classroom noise by special arrangements (e.g. having carpeted classrooms or soundproofing) is sometimes possible in specialist settings, though this is beyond the scope of most mainstream schools.

- **Smell**

  - Raising staff awareness that some children with ASD may find some smells distressing such as perfumes/deodorants or materials in classrooms like paints/glue/cleaning fluids. Find suitable alternatives for materials with strong odours where possible.

  - Allowing the child to work in a different area if activities involve strong-smelling materials may help. Encouraging the child to eat in a suitable area of the dining hall if the child dislikes the smell of cooked food (e.g. seating them near a door or window) can also be useful.

  - Highlighting that it is not only smells which come from the school itself which can be problematic: a child may be sensitive to strong smells from outside the classroom (e.g. traffic fumes, farm smells).

- **Touch and feel**

  - Distracting sensory issues can arise when children find their clothing or uniform uncomfortable. This can be strongly unpleasant for them. In these cases allow for flexibility with adherence to school uniform rules (e.g. adapting the uniform to the child's needs may involve small modifications, such as cutting the labels out of their uniform).

  - Raising awareness that some pupils might be 'touch-averse', in which case make special allowances for children to opt out of certain activities (e.g. holding hands, playing tag, some games in PE).

  - Being aware that sometimes the attention and concentration of children with ASD can be disrupted because of their special requirements regarding stimuli they find distressing. Seating should be comfortable (e.g. if a pupil is sitting on the floor then they should be allowed to sit on a carpet square rather than directly on the floor).

  - Considering issues such as the fact that the texture of food may be a problem at lunch times or in cookery lessons can be helpful. The child may not enjoy the sensation of getting his/her hands messy in practical subjects such as cookery or art, so modifications may have to be made. For example, this child might not be involved in touching messy foods, but in chopping or mixing the dry foods instead.

  - Challenging behaviour in the classroom can be alleviated by the use of a stress ball or a piece of material in a texture which the child likes. This can help a child who has been behaving in a distracted manner to relax and resume classroom activities. For example Blu-Tack or a piece of soft fabric could be used (see Appendix 22, Relaxation Strategies).

CAUTION

Occupational therapy

For some children, sensory issues can have a significant impact on their functioning and wellbeing so in these cases implementing specific sensory programmes may be required. Wherever possible consult an occupational therapist.

Possible risk of bullying

It is important to carefully consider the implications of some strategies and discuss these with the child and their parents/carers. Whilst some of the strategies are effective in minimising distress and discomfort caused by sensory sensitivity, they may inevitably highlight differences (e.g. if the child is wearing headphones or having a different lesson structure). This could leave the child more vulnerable to bullying and it is essential that appropriate steps are taken to avoid this.

Hypo-sensitivity to pain

Some children might accidentally wound themselves and not bring it to anyone's attention because they may feel less pain than other children. If the child is hypo-sensitive to pain then this should be highlighted to other staff members.

FINAL CONSIDERATIONS

In preparing for the transition to secondary school, perhaps one of the most important facts of which teachers need to be cognisant is that behaviour which may at times appear inappropriate and unusual is often a result of the sensory issues of the child with ASD. Making use of some of the recommendations in this chapter can help to prevent misinterpretation of the child's actions as well as ameliorating the discomfort, anxiety and challenging behaviour which sensory issues can cause.

In addition, many children with ASD can also have specific sensory interests which can be utilised in the following positive ways:

- **As a reward**

  If a child enjoys the sensory stimulation something produces, then this can be used as a 'reward' for coping with tasks they find demanding or challenging. After agreement and planning with the child, specific times can be scheduled in their timetable for them to engage in their sensory interests in a private area as a reward (e.g. spinning colourful discs, playing with squeeze toys or soft pieces of cloth (see Appendix 17, Sensory Equipment).

- **As a calming activity/strategy**

  Some children with ASD can find engaging in their sensory interests very soothing and therefore this can be used as a helpful calming activity. This can be particularly helpful for children who have difficulties with anxiety or stress management. In these instances creating a 'de-stress toolkit' which contains favourite sensory items and agreeing upon times and places these can be used is recommended. This should be kept in a set place for the child to access (e.g. a form room) (see Appendix 17, Sensory Equipment as well as Chapter 4 on Difficulties with Imagination and Flexible Thinking, Chapter 8 on Anxiety and Chapter 9 on Challenging Behaviour).

CHAPTER 8

ANXIETY

WHY IS THIS IMPORTANT?

Children with ASD are at much higher risk than their typically developing peers of developing problems with anxiety or even anxiety disorders. In fact, research indicates that as many as 50–80% of children with ASD have at least one, and often several types, of anxiety disorder.

Anxiety is a significant problem for children with ASD for a number of reasons. Although we do not yet fully understand the causes of anxiety in people with ASD from the neurobiological point of view, psychological and environmental factors play a considerable role. ASD as a condition predisposes children to experience higher levels of stress due to its inherent impairments in areas such as adapting to change, understanding the social environment or predicting causal events. Many books about ASD often make an analogy about its impact being like travelling to a foreign country and feeling insecure and confused as a result of difficulty understanding the language, culture, customs or how things work. There are also secondary consequences often associated with ASD which exacerbate anxiety and stress, such as an increased risk of social isolation, exploitation or bullying.

High anxiety tends to have a major impact on a child's ability to function in daily life and on their psychological wellbeing. For example, high levels of stress and anxiety are found to significantly affect a child's ability to concentrate and consequently may lead to academic underachievement. It also tends to result in the child avoiding new, even exciting, situations and thus limits their learning opportunities. In addition, it can lead to behavioural difficulties and in extreme cases to school avoidance.

WHAT DO WE NEED TO KNOW ABOUT ANXIETY IN ASD?

How can we identify anxiety in children with ASD?

Children with ASD have difficulty expressing their feelings both verbally and nonverbally. They may struggle to talk openly about their worries, even when encouraged.

Furthermore, as children with ASD have problems with nonverbal communication, symptoms of anxiety may not even be obvious through facial expression, tone of voice or body language (e.g. a lot of children with ASD may have the same fixed smile on their face both when they are nervous or relaxed). As a result, there is a significant risk of underestimating the intensity of the child's anxiety.

Many children are also able to disguise their anxiety symptoms at school, only to have emotional 'meltdowns' when they return home. Thus, it is important to highlight that a lot of children with ASD can present very differently in the school and home environments. This can cause the adults around the child to have very discrepant views about the nature and intensity of the child's problems. Some teachers even report that it can almost be difficult to believe that the child is experiencing the extreme anxiety reported by the parents until they have had an opportunity to witness it first-hand.

Elements which are invaluable in identifying possible difficulties with anxiety are an awareness that pupils with ASD are at increased risk of developing anxiety problems or disorders, monitoring the child's behaviour and noting any changes (e.g. increase in repetitive questioning or withdrawal from activities which the child used to enjoy) and close communication with the family.

What triggers anxiety?

Different things make different children anxious. Some anxiety triggers may be directly associated with ASD itself, whilst other causes may be secondary consequences of ASD, or related to previous negative experiences. For some children, anxiety can be an issue with which they may need continuous support, whilst for others it may just be temporarily increased as a result of significant changes linked with the transition to secondary school. In order to adapt strategies appropriately, it is important to identify the triggers:

- **Triggers associated with transition to secondary school:** As many children with ASD find change difficult, a step as significant as the transition to secondary school can often be very anxiety provoking. Pupils can be particularly worried about changes in routine, expectations or new social situations (e.g. having to meet many new children and teachers). Some pupils tend to worry about environmental changes (e.g. size of the school or getting lost). Many children with ASD have a tendency towards perfectionism and black-and-white thinking. Consequently, this often results in intense anticipatory anxiety about unintentionally breaking some rules or getting detention, even if there may not be an obvious rationale for the pupil to worry about this.

- **Triggers associated with ASD:** Many diagnostic features of ASD can directly or indirectly exacerbate the child's anxiety levels. One of the common anxiety triggers is sensory over-sensitivity (e.g. worrying about noise in the corridor) or anticipatory anxiety prior to any change to routine (e.g. worrying about having a supply teacher or about a forthcoming school trip). Unstructured times, such as breaks or lunch time, can also be anxiety provoking, as children with ASD often worry about not being able to initiate any activities or not having any friends with whom they can sit.

- **Triggers associated with previous negative experiences:** Children with ASD, similar to children with other disabilities, are at increased risk of encountering negative life events such as social isolation, bullying or perceived 'failure'. This can be related either to their ASD or to other comorbid difficulties. For example, children who also have dyspraxia are often particularly scared of PE or sports days as they anticipate being laughed at or never being picked for the team. A lot of children with ASD tend to have difficulties with organisation and consequently worry about forgetting their homework or being told off for things they have done unintentionally.

How to identify anxiety triggers

Awareness of the possible sources of anxiety for children with ASD can be very helpful in correctly interpreting the child's behaviour and in identifying its triggers. In addition, communication with parents is often an invaluable source of information about the child's possible anxiety, as many children feel able to express their concerns only in the 'safe' home environment. Taking time to establish regular contact with the family and obtain their feedback about the child's wellbeing is therefore very worthwhile. It is also important to remember that children with ASD can present very differently in different environments. Even if the child does not express their worries at school, parental concerns should be taken seriously.

 HOW CAN WE HELP?

The key to reducing the pupil's anxiety is to accurately identify the cause. Below are proactive strategies aimed at addressing the triggers of anxiety. This is the first-line approach. Second, strategies aimed at promoting coping skills for pupils for whom this is a more persistent problem are covered:

- **Proactive strategies:** prevention of triggers

- **Management strategies:** expanding the child's coping skills.

Proactive strategies: prevention of triggers

- **Anxiety caused by difficulties with change**
  Uncertainty and anxiety arise when children with ASD struggle to understand their surroundings due to environmental changes or changes in routine. Anxiety can be reduced by creating predictability using the following strategies:

  - **Gradual familiarisation:** Children with ASD who are particularly worried about change often benefit from gradual familiarisation with the new environment and its rules. This may involve a visit to the new school prior to transition or getting to meet at least one 'allocated' member of staff. Please refer to Chapter 1, General Support with Transition to Secondary School, for more in-depth information about relevant strategies.

  - **Planning ahead:** Being prepared in advance tends to increase the child's ability to cope with change and typically reduces anticipatory anxiety. Children will benefit from knowing what is going to happen, but will also need details such as what is expected of them, who will be involved, and what to do when they get stuck. Using visual strategies, such as timetables or advance 'warning' in a diary, can be particularly effective because children can refer to the visual record whenever they get anxious. Their parents can also use the materials to reassure the child. Please refer to Chapter 4, Difficulties with Imagination and Flexible Thinking for more in-depth information about support strategies.

■ **Managing transition:** Transitions in general, even minor ones like moving from one activity to another, can be a source of anxiety for children with ASD, for a number of reasons. This may be because they struggle with flexibility of thinking and shifting their attention between different activities, or because of the organisational demands involved. As a result, the child may not be able to keep up with their peers, or may end up at a loss as to where to go or what to do. If this is likely to be a sensitive issue for the pupil, implementing external prompting and structure can help to prepare the child and reduce their last-minute panic. Strategies such as advance notification, countdowns, giving reminders when the transition is approaching (e.g. 5 minutes prior to the end of the activity) can all assist the child in transitioning appropriately. Other strategies which are known to be useful include using a timer (e.g. when the child is engaged in their special interest) and providing the child with a checklist of the things needed for the next activity. Please refer to Chapter 4, Difficulties with Imagination and Flexible Thinking, for more in-depth information about support strategies.

■ **Anxiety caused by social difficulties**

Fear of being isolated, unliked, excluded or bullied is very prevalent amongst children with ASD. It often stems from a child's awareness of their social difficulties and sadly, also from their previous negative experiences. In addition, not being able to interpret verbal and nonverbal communication increases uncertainty and makes social situations more confusing. Meeting new people can therefore be a very stressful experience for a young person with ASD. In more serious instances, children can develop social phobia or avoidance of social situations, which requires specialist treatment. However, in most cases, having a structured social setting can be beneficial in supporting children in developing positive social relationships and experiences, as well as increasing their confidence in social situations. This can be achieved through implementing the following strategies:

■ **Promoting social understanding:** This is especially useful for pupils who tend to be predominantly anxious about not knowing how to start conversations or join in with others. There is a range of useful resources that can be used to teach children social skills. In some schools there are opportunities for pupils to join social skills groups. If this is not possible, the personalised resources listed in Chapter 2, Social Interaction, and the respective appendices can be adapted for the pupil. This can include the use of Social Stories around issues which are particularly difficult for the pupil, or explicitly teaching the pupil how to engage in conversations or join a group.

■ **Facilitating social inclusion:** Organising structured social activities during the breaks in the school day is a great opportunity for children with social communication difficulties to meet and integrate with like-minded pupils, enabling social inclusion and potential friendships. There can be different formats for structuring opportunities to integrate with peers, ranging from open lunch time clubs (where children can come in whenever they wish) or interest groups to one-on-one mentoring, buddy systems or Circle of Friends, which would require skilled adult facilitation. Please refer to Chapter 2, Social Interaction, for more detailed information about these support strategies.

- **Preventing bullying:** Both government guidelines and research studies recommend that the whole school approach and zero tolerance of bullying are the most effective ways of managing this very complex and difficult issue. Creating an awareness that despite best efforts, bullying does occur, and encouraging and reinforcing the reporting of any bullying incidents are the first steps in eliminating the problem. However, children with ASD may need more support than their peers with reporting and managing bullying (e.g. knowing who to talk to and when, or how to explain complex social situations leading up to bullying). Children with ASD may also present with specific behaviours which may increase their risk of being bullied (e.g. the need to adhere to rules so strongly that they correct their peers in the absence of their teacher), or they may have difficulties with understanding and interpreting the behaviour of their peers (e.g. some children with ASD can misinterpret another child accidentally bumping into them as intentional bullying). Prevention of bullying for children with ASD therefore brings with it specific challenges that may require additional consideration. Combining one-to-one support aimed at empowering the pupil with ASD, working with the wider peer network around the role of bystanders to bullying and managing environmental factors (e.g. identifying the most vulnerable times) is recommended. Please refer to Chapter 5, Bullying, for more detailed information about useful support strategies.

- **Anxiety caused by sensory sensitivities**
The ways in which children with ASD experience sensory stimuli can be markedly different from those of their peers. They can either be over-sensitive or experience reduced sensitivity to sensory stimuli. Sensory sensitivities can include problems involving visual stimuli, noise, sound, taste, smell and touch. Whilst not all children with ASD are affected by sensory issues, for those who are, it can be one of their primary difficulties and sources of distress. Some children and adults with ASD even report it as being physically painful. As this is not something over which children with ASD have control, ensuring proactive support is paramount.

- **Environmental strategies:** Once the sensory issue is identified, proactive measures can be taken to reduce its impact on the pupil. For example, minimising auditory or visual distractions (e.g. reducing the humming and flickering of fluorescent lights), considering seating arrangements, providing suitable alternatives for activities pupils may find distressing due to their sensory loading (e.g. allowing pupils to eat in a quiet area instead of the canteen if they are over-sensitive to noise) or adjusting materials if appropriate (e.g. using odour-free glue) should all be considered. Whenever possible, using environmental alternatives is preferable, as it does not single out the pupil in any way, yet can often be very effective. Please refer to the Chapter 7, Sensory Sensitivities, for more detailed information about support strategies.

- **Individualised strategies:** Occasionally, some pupils with ASD can experience more intense reactions to certain sensory stimuli, the impact of which may not be possible to fully eliminate via general environmental measures. In these instances, consideration should be given to specific aides that could be used. For example, pupils could benefit from using headphones (or earplugs) when in noisy areas such as canteens. Alternatively, special arrangements should be granted to accommodate the pupil's tactile aversiveness (e.g. allowing the child to substitute parts of the uniform). Please refer to Chapter 7, Sensory Sensitivities, for more detailed information about support strategies.

- **Anxiety caused by additional difficulties and fear of failure**
  Children with ASD are at increased risk of having additional (so-called comorbid) neurodevelopmental conditions. This includes developmental coordination disorder (otherwise known as dyspraxia), which is associated with clumsiness, tic disorders or Tourette syndrome (which presents with noticeable motor and/or vocal tics), or other conditions. Please refer to Chapter 10, Conditions that Co-Occur with ASD, for more detailed information. Comorbid difficulties tend to exacerbate the child's feeling of being different and can often be a source of intense embarrassment and can create a fear of humiliation. These concerns are not unfounded. Research indicates that children with ASD who also have with motor coordination difficulties are much more likely to be bullied and socially isolated than their more agile and athletic peers with the same diagnosis.

  - **Awareness:** Unfortunately these difficulties often go undiagnosed and untreated despite the awareness that children with ASD are at risk of having other related disorders. Teachers often play an invaluable role in noticing a child's problems as they frequently have a lot more in-depth knowledge of the child than mental health professionals. Increasing the awareness of staff that they should monitor a pupil's presentation can therefore be invaluable in both detecting possible comorbid difficulties and responding to those sensitively.

  - **Individualised modifications:** Once a difficulty is identified, it can be very reassuring for the pupil to have a clear plan about adaptations that can be made. For example, children with motor coordination problems tend to experience high levels of anxiety about PE, about always being the last one to be picked for a team, or about letting the team down by missing a goal. In this situation, it might be helpful for the teacher to think of alternative ways of picking team members, such as by assigning numbers 1 and 2 and asking them to get into groups. In order for the plan of modification to be successful in reducing anxiety, it is important to be thoughtful and thorough about different aspects of the school day that demand a given skill. For the pupil with dyspraxia, this may not only be the time during the PE lesson itself, but also at other times (e.g. in the changing rooms, due to difficulty getting changed at the same pace as peers).

- **Anxiety caused by organisational problems**
  Most young people with ASD struggle with organisation and planning. Difficulties with planning and organisation can impact on academic work (e.g. homework) and other day-to-day activities (e.g. moving between classrooms). Young people with ASD have described these difficulties, such as forgetting their homework or getting lost in the new school building, as being very embarrassing and stressful. If needed, it is important to provide pupils with strategies to help them plan and organise their daily activities in order to reduce their anxiety.

- **Understanding:** Most pupils with organisational and planning problems are particularly anxious about 'getting into trouble' and appearing as if they did not try their best. For example, children often report that they worry that they have not completed homework satisfactorily because they have not been able to write down the assignment or they have misunderstood it. It is therefore helpful to be aware that children with ASD are likely to have these difficulties and it is important to use strategies aimed at helping them address the underlying problem. This will provide pupils with a reassuring feeling of being understood by the teacher and will reduce their anxiety about receiving sanctions, since their errors are not intentional.

- **Organisation of materials:** Pupils with ASD find it significantly more difficult than most of their peers to organise themselves independently and in the absence of external support will hence be more likely to forget their homework or bring the wrong material to class. To support these pupils, strategies can be implemented both to provide them with external reminders and prompts, as well as to help them to gradually work on their organisational skills. Having a consistent structure to the strategies is the key, as over time it will become more habitual for the pupil to use this system with a decreasing amount of external prompting. For example, the young person should be encouraged to use a homework diary. The pupil may benefit from a checklist of things to bring for the day or colour-coded timetables with corresponding colours on the materials for each subject (e.g. red is used for maths on the timetable as well as for the maths folder or book). Please see Chapter 6, Planning and Organisation Problems, for more detailed support strategies. If homework is a particular area of concern for the pupil, please refer to Chapter 1, General Support with Transition to Secondary School.

- **Moving between classrooms:** Moving between classrooms can be a very stressful experience for young people with ASD. Not only can it be difficult to remember where to go in a big new building, but one also has to move through corridors which can be overwhelming in terms of the numbers of other students, the physical closeness to them, and the amount of noise. Providing the student with a clear map of the school building (e.g. mark the classrooms, dining hall and other locations on it for them, perhaps in colour) can be particularly helpful for pupils with good visual-spatial skills, which is often a strength for children with ASD. If the child finds it difficult to transition between classrooms in a noisy corridor then it may be helpful to let them make the transition a couple of minutes before end of class in the first few weeks of term. Whilst this may be sufficient for most children, some pupils may need more intensive or long-term support, such as aided transition between classrooms (e.g. a peer or staff member takes the child to the various classrooms).

Proactive strategies: expanding the child's coping skills

- **Helping the child to communicate their anxiety or worries effectively**
  Pupils with ASD find it more difficult than their peers to effectively communicate their worries and concerns. This is partly explained by the fact that children with ASD often have significant difficulty with insight into their own emotions and/or communicating their emotions verbally or nonverbally. Hence there is a risk that the level of anxiety the child is experiencing is underestimated. Furthermore, by the time pupils have approached the transition to secondary school they are at risk of having developed a sense of 'learned helplessness', arising from their negative past experiences (i.e. a perception of themselves as unable to succeed or alter their situation regardless of how much they try).

  - **Emotional literacy:** Emotional literacy refers to the ability of the young person to understand their own emotions and those of others. Time spent developing and teaching emotional literacy has been found to be very effective in helping children deal with anxieties and worries. A basic principle in teaching the child about emotions is to explore individual feelings one at a time (e.g. happiness, anxiety) in terms of facial expression, tone of voice, body language and context. The aim is to help the child identify triggers and physiological responses to anxiety in order for them to learn to cope with their anxiety. This will enable the young person to identify their own cues more easily. It might then be helpful to use a visual representation of the intensity of the emotion, such as an emotional thermometer (see Appendix 14), which helps the child understand their own emotions, but also to more readily communicate them appropriately.

  - **Communication of feelings:** As mentioned above, a child with ASD will often struggle with communicating their emotions, and visual external strategies have been found to be very useful. For example, it has been found to be helpful to provide the child with an 'anxiety alert card' to indicate that they are feeling anxious. This can be a small card that the child can either discreetly shows the teacher or place on their desk when feeling overwhelmed (see Appendix 11). Clear rules need to be established as to when and how the card is used. Depending on the individual child, it may either be agreed that the child can leave the classroom for five minutes or that the teacher approaches the child to discuss the child's concerns. It is very important that all members of staff are aware of the purpose of the card to prevent staff from thinking that the card is used to avoid the lesson. Furthermore, the emotional thermometer (Appendix 14) may be helpful tool to communicate the intensity of the feelings.

- **Safe haven**
  For children with high levels of anxiety, it can be very reassuring to identify a secure place, where they can go to calm down and seek security. This can be any place in which the child feels comfortable and safe (e.g. the library). Children with ASD really benefit from clear guidelines as where to go and who to speak to when they feel anxious, worried or unhappy.

- **Relaxation techniques**
  Utilising relaxation strategies can help a child with ASD who finds it very difficult to relax. It is important that children with ASD learn arousal regulation and relaxation skills in order to empower them to independently reduce the anxiety they are experiencing (see Appendix 22).

There is no one way of relaxing and it might be helpful to try out different relaxation methods that might be helpful for the child.

- **Emotional toolbox:** Engaging in relaxing activities can ease feelings of anxiety and anger in all of us. A child with ASD may struggle to independently identify the activities that can have this positive effect. It is therefore important to explore collaboratively with the child different types of activities that can help 'repair' feelings of anxiety for that child, for example, playing with a stress ball, engaging in their special interest for a limited amount of time, reading a book, talking to a friend, or spending some time in a quiet room. It can be helpful to draw a toolbox and write in all the tools that repair feelings of anxiety (see Appendices 15 and 22).

- **Breathing exercises:** Controlled breathing is a method of relaxation with the primary goal being to slow breathing down. It is a method that can be used discreetly at any time. The child should be encouraged to take a deep breath and hold it for five seconds and then slowly breathe out. This should be repeated a couple of times.

CAUTION

If increased anxiety is suspected and there are concerns regarding this, these should be discussed with the parent and advice given to consult the child's GP regarding a possible referral to a child and adolescent psychiatrist or psychologist via the local CAMHS (Child and Adolescent Mental Health Services), if appropriate. Please see Chapter 10, Conditions that Co-Occur with ASD.

FINAL CONSIDERATIONS

As many children with ASD suffer from anxiety it is important that teaching staff are aware that this can be a big issue affecting all aspects of the child's school experience. By implementing useful strategies that have been suggested this can ameliorate the stress experienced, therefore helping the child in many other areas of school life. Being less stressed may allow them to function more fully and be able to reach their full academic and social potential. Often children with ASD in mainstream settings are cognitively able and by supporting them in various ways, including how to reduce and manage their anxiety, this will contribute greatly to their emotional wellbeing and allow them to get the most from their experience of school.

CHAPTER 9

CHALLENGING BEHAVIOUR

WHY IS THIS IMPORTANT?

Behaviours are considered 'challenging' when they lie outside the conventional limits of what is considered acceptable, whilst also carrying significant risks to the wellbeing of a child with ASD and/or those around them. Challenging behaviour is not part of ASD – but it is more common in children with the disorder. It usually arises in response to communication difficulties and feelings of confusion and powerlessness. Examples of challenging behaviour which might be seen at school include arguing with teachers, refusing to comply with instructions, damaging property, being aggressive towards staff and peers, self-injury and having tantrums. Tackling challenging behaviour is often a high priority for teachers, as, left unmanaged, it can disrupt the learning and progress not only of children with ASD but potentially that of their classmates as well.

WHAT DO WE NEED TO KNOW ABOUT CHALLENGING BEHAVIOUR?

Defining challenging behaviour

Challenging behaviours have two important characteristics. First, they are outside conventional norms for acceptable behaviour. In education, they involve breaking school rules and going against the values of the school. Second, they pose some risk to the person carrying out the behaviour and/or to other people. This risk can be physical – for example when a boy with ASD puts himself, his peers and his teacher at risk of an injury during a severe tantrum. However, it is important to recognise that this risk can also be more subtle – as when a child risks social exclusion due to regularly swearing at other pupils; or when he misses out on learning because he frequently argues with teachers, resulting in his removal from lessons.

Challenging behaviours in ASD – a means of communication

Philip Whitaker (2001) has written that challenging behaviours in ASD are the 'tip of the iceberg' – meaning that they indicate there is a lot more going on under the surface. People with ASD face more difficulties at school than most, as this environment places great demands on their social capacities, their communication and their ability to be flexible. These demands often lead to confusion, frustration and anxiety, which the person with ASD then finds difficult to express or even identify. Challenging behaviour in ASD can often be understood in this context. So, when a child with ASD has a tantrum or refuses to cooperate, it might be their way of saying 'I'm tired', or 'I'm frightened' or 'I don't understand'. This means that when we see challenging behaviour in someone with ASD, we can better understand what is going on under the surface by asking 'What is this child trying to tell me?'

Challenging behaviour in ASD – a way of taking control

Many people with ASD have a strong need for certainty and control, yet their difficulties mean that they are frequently unsure about what is happening and what will happen next. It is important to recognise that some challenging behaviours are an attempt to take control of a situation. Therefore, when trying to understand a behavioural problem, it is helpful to ask 'What is the purpose of this behaviour?' and 'What is the child trying to achieve?'

CAUTION

Challenging behaviour and children with special needs

Few people are more expert than teachers at dealing with challenging behaviour. Often the skills they have developed will be just right for dealing with the behavioural problems of pupils with ASD. However, it must be acknowledged that children with ASD will sometimes have challenging behaviours which arise from their specific difficulties. At these times allowances will need to be made for an individual's ASD. For example, a child with ASD who has challenging behaviour due to sensory overload in a noisy, brightly lit classroom may need regular breaks in a calm area, and would not benefit from strategies used with typically developing pupils with a superficially similar behaviour. In fact, conventional strategies could make matters worse by making the child more stressed and overwhelmed.

HOW CAN WE HELP?

Pupils with ASD can be helped by modifying their environment to remove the triggers and incentives associated with their challenging behaviour. Also, they can be taught new skills that make them feel less confused and more in control. The following are described below:

- **Proactive strategies:** removing the triggers for challenging behaviour
- **Management strategies:** addressing challenging behaviour and its causes.

Proactive Strategies: removing the triggers for challenging behaviour

- **Communication**

  If teachers can enhance both their understanding of the child's communication, and the child's understanding of their communication, the risk of there being an episode of challenging behaviour will be greatly reduced. The tips below are useful in that they help to compensate for difficulties with taking language literally and processing language slowly (see also Chapter 3, Language Difficulties):

  - Rather than telling the child what not to do, tell them what they should do instead.

  - Verbal information needs to be direct and literal (e.g. 'sit down please' rather than 'would you mind sitting down').

  - Avoid ambiguities such as 'maybe'. Instead say, 'I don't know yet. I will find out after the break'.

  - Avoid abstract terms such as 'calm down'. Instead aim to give the child something specific to do, such as breathing exercises.

  - Avoid asking open-ended questions, but give the child a choice between two or three short answers.

  - Humour can be helpful for some children, but be mindful that the child may interpret jokes literally; irony and sarcasm can be particularly confusing to a person with ASD.

- **Planning ahead**

  A child with ASD may have trouble predicting day-to-day activities and find it difficult to adapt to changes in their routine. This can result in anxiety, anger, confusion – and challenging behaviour. These strategies aim to provide certainty, which is known to help pupils with ASD to feel secure (see also Chapter 6, Planning and Organisation Problems).

  - Provide a clear structure to the day, including when and with whom activities will take place.

  - Prepare a clear, personalised timetable (see Appendix 10).

  - Use visual reminders to warn the child of changes to their routine. For example, a visit to a museum could be preceded by a countdown involving crossing off days on a calendar.

  - Colour code books, materials and timetables for subjects and location of classes.

  - Provide prompt cards for upcoming transitions. If changing activities in five minutes, a prearranged visual cue from the teacher may be useful.

  - Prompt cards can also be used for 'what-if' situations (e.g. feeling ill or arriving late) (see Appendix 11).

  - Mark the ending of tasks clearly and explicitly before moving on.

- **Managing break times**

  Young people with ASD often find unstructured times, such as break, difficult and this can lead to challenging behaviour. Often this arises from their confusion and anxiety, or simply their uncertainty as to how to behave. The following strategies can help with these difficulties, and so should reduce challenging behaviour that occurs in break times (see also Chapter 6, Planning and Organisation Problems).

  - Agree with the child a safe place they can go to if they need to.

  - Also prearrange a dedicated person to go to if needed during break times. Try to ensure that this person is consistent (i.e. not a different individual every time) and that they really are available when the child seeks them out.

  - Organised lunch time activities that provide structure can be a great relief to children with ASD. This could include lunch time clubs dedicated to board games, drama, films and so on. If these are available, they should be explicitly included in the child's timetable (see Appendices 10 and 12).

  - Implement a buddy system if the child wants, but struggles to find, companionship during breaks (see Appendix 13).

- **Managing sensory stimuli**

  Young people with ASD can be overwhelmed by sensations that most people barely notice – such as the noise of a lively classroom or the flickering of strip lighting. This sensory overload can arise from certain sounds, lighting or even textures. This can impact on mood and give rise to challenging behaviour. For example, a young person with ASD may not turn up to class because they find it difficult to transition between one lesson and another due to crowded and noisy corridors; or they may leave the lessons without permission when classroom noise becomes intolerable to them.

  It is important to identify if the young person has sensory difficulties and exactly what these difficulties are. Then, creative solutions can be negotiated. Sometimes this will involve making an exception for the child by relaxing school rules (see also Chapter 7, Sensory Sensitivities).

  Here are some examples of helpful strategies to counter the effects of sensory overload:

  - If the child finds it difficult to transition between classrooms in a noisy corridor, let them make the transition a couple of minutes before the end of class. This may not need to be a permanent strategy, as it might only be necessary in the first weeks of term. Provide the child with a 'time-out' card with clear rules about when to use it. The child should leave the classroom when they feel overwhelmed (see Chapter 7, Sensory Sensitivities, and Appendix 11).

  - Provide a physical space where the child can escape sensations that overwhelm them.

  - Consider the seating of the pupil. For example, you could put them near a door or window if they are averse to smells, or away from a window if strong light is too much for them.

Management strategies: addressing challenging behaviour and its causes

■ **Building social communication capacities**

Often challenging behaviour can result from difficulties understanding and using language and/or difficulties with social interaction. Work can be done with the child to enhance their social communication skills, using for example Social Stories, which are described in Appendix 8. This involves using cartoons to explain everyday situations and appropriate behaviour. Keep in mind that these stories should not be presented while the child is showing the challenging behaviour. Instead the stories can be used during a calm moment in the day and repeated over time. (See also Chapter 2, Social Interaction and Chapter 3, Language Difficulties.)

■ **Emotional regulation**

Challenging behaviour in ASD often arises from strong, unmanageable emotions – so we need to help children with behavioural problems to express and regulate their feelings in more constructive, socially appropriate ways. The first step towards this involves helping them better recognise and understand their emotions. Once they can do this, they will have less need to express their distress using challenging behaviour. We suggest two techniques for enhancing emotional understanding and regulation:

■ **Emotional thermometer:** Teach the child to use an emotional thermometer to help them understand their feelings. They can then use this tool to communicate about the nature and intensity of their feelings (see Appendix 14).

■ **Emotional toolbox:** Explore together with the child which tools/strategies could be helpful to repair feelings of anger or anxiety. This will lead to increased self-efficacy to master their emotions (see Appendix 15).

■ **Tackling challenging behaviour**

It will not always be possible to eliminate a challenging behaviour simply by improving the fit between a child's capacities and the demands placed on them by the school environment. In these cases, an active approach is required, involving detailed analysis of what triggers the behaviour, and what consequences the behaviour has that mean the child continues to repeat it. This approach will now be described in a step-by-step manner, based on the guidelines offered by Zarkowska & Clements (1994) for their STAR system. The STAR system is summarised in Figure 9.1.

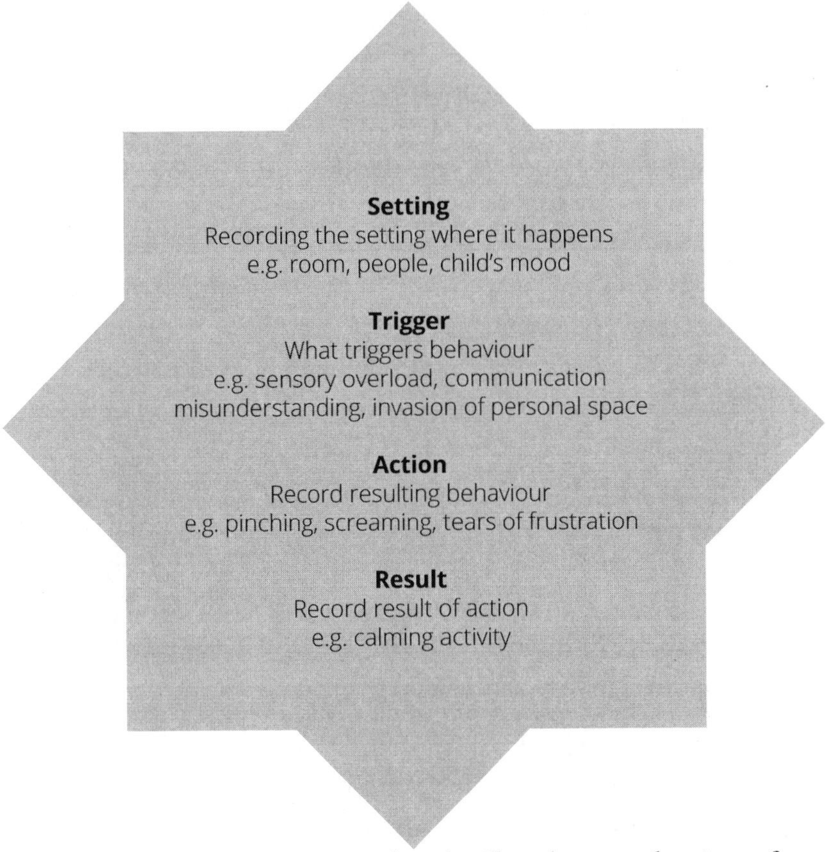

Setting
Recording the setting where it happens
e.g. room, people, child's mood

Trigger
What triggers behaviour
e.g. sensory overload, communication
misunderstanding, invasion of personal space

Action
Record resulting behaviour
e.g. pinching, screaming, tears of frustration

Result
Record result of action
e.g. calming activity

Figure 9.1: The STAR system used to identify and manage the triggers for challenging behaviour (Zarkowska and Clements, 1994)

- **Step one:** It is essential that the problem behaviour is clearly defined. Be specific and concrete. For example do not choose 'misbehaving in class' as a problem behaviour. Instead aim for target behaviours like 'gets up from desk and leaves room during lessons' or 'repeatedly bangs on desk with hands'. When tackling problem behaviours, pick one at a time, rather than trying to work on several at once.

- **Step two:** Collect information on the behaviour using the STAR system. This should be done using the table in Appendix 16, and must include information about several incidents of the challenging behaviour.

- **Step three:** Analyse the information in the STAR table. This is where you need to come up with some ideas about what is causing and maintaining the behaviour. Here are some useful questions to help guide this process:

  - When is the behaviour most likely to happen?

  - Where is the behaviour most likely to happen?

  - With whom is the behaviour most likely to happen?

  - What activity is most likely to produce the behaviour?

- What other situations can produce the behaviour?

- What might the person have been feeling when they started the behaviour?

- Had they eaten and slept enough?

- Was the behaviour associated with a change in routine or a transition between activities?

- What are the exceptions – are there times when it does not happen?

- What is gained by engaging in the behaviour?

- What is avoided by engaging in the behaviour?

- Is the behaviour communicating something that the child struggles to say?

- What does the child enjoy doing?

- What would motivate them to behave differently?

- What skills does the child have that could replace the function of the behaviour?

- **Step four:** After going through the information in the STAR table and asking the above questions, the teacher will have some hunches as to what causes and maintains the problem behaviour. These will provide the teacher with some ideas about what can be done to reduce the problem behaviour. These ideas should involve some or all of the following basic strategies:

  - Removing triggers for the behaviour

  - Rewarding the child for alternative, appropriate behaviours

  - Ensuring that the challenging behaviour is not rewarded when it does occur.

Below are some of the ways in which these strategies can be put in place:

- **Time-out cards:** These help children to manage their own environment, and therefore to remove the triggers for problem behaviour. They enable them to effectively communicate to the teacher when they are becoming overwhelmed or stressed, and are in danger of showing challenging behaviour. When carried out appropriately, 'time out' can provide the child with the opportunity to calm down by limiting external stimulation (see Appendix 11).

- **Redirecting behaviour:** Redirecting the child's attention to a preferred topic of conversation or activity can be an extremely effective way of preventing a situation getting worse or of diffusing a difficult situation. Using the STAR sheet you will have a good feel for the kinds of things that will trigger certain behaviour. Use relaxation strategies and anger management techniques (see Appendix 22).

- **Planned ignoring:** This strategy involves ignoring undesirable behaviour, but not necessarily ignoring the child when they are doing it. This can be effective because responses provided by others, such as giving attention or providing an object or activity, may be maintaining an unwanted type of behaviour, even without staff realising it. Planned ignoring involves providing no response to the behaviour, including verbal comments, body language, facial expression or eye contact. This needs to be coupled with other strategies such as positive reinforcement to give the child an opportunity to learn alternative ways of achieving what they want. In other words, for this to work, you need to be ready to respond to and reinforce the child's appropriate behaviour as well as withdrawing the response to inappropriate behaviour.

- **Punishment:** Lots of research has shown that this strategy does not work. It's not an effective way to promote learning because the cause of the problem is not addressed.

- **Detention:** A lot of children are worried about getting detentions in secondary school. It is important that all staff are aware of the child's difficulties to ensure that the child does not get into trouble for behaviour that cannot be helped, since it reflects their ASD. This is particularly important, as the current White Paper from the Department of Education abolishes the requirement for 24 hours' notice for detention (House of Commons Education Committee, 2011).

FINAL CONSIDERATIONS

Challenging behaviour at school is a sign that there is a mismatch between the child and the school environment. It often reflects a child's inability to understand or communicate about this mismatch, and can represent an attempt to take control of a frightening, frustrating and confusing situation. By thinking about what causes and maintains a child's problem behaviours, we often learn a lot about that child, including how better to support them in education. Using the STAR system described above should help teachers to understand the causes of a specific individual's challenging behaviour, and to generate ways to address it. Helping with challenging behaviour involves removing its triggers, changing the way people respond to the behaviour, and/or providing the child with new skills and ways to communicate.

CHAPTER 10

CONDITIONS THAT CO-OCCUR WITH ASD

WHY IS THIS IMPORTANT?

Research indicates that children with ASD are at significantly increased risk of having additional developmental problems, such as ADHD, or mental health and emotional difficulties, such as anxiety, depression or conduct problems. When such conditions co-occur with ASD, we call this 'comorbidity'. There is still a debate about the exact prevalence rates of these comorbid difficulties. All studies are consistent in reporting that 70–87% of children with ASD meet criteria for at least one additional diagnosis and it is not unusual for children with ASD to have several co-existing diagnoses at the same time.

Many children do not have a formal diagnosis for their additional difficulties, hence their impact may be underestimated. This is often because children with ASD may not be as good at describing their emotional states verbally or nonverbally, or because people around them attribute their difficulties to their diagnosis of ASD (so-called 'diagnostic overshadowing'). In many cases, the co-existing mental health or developmental problems have a detrimental impact on the child's functioning.

Comorbid conditions frequently lead to exacerbation of the child's ASD symptomatology (e.g. social withdrawal and an increase in repetitive behaviour). Their impact may be particularly noticeable in the classroom, whereby the child may present with challenging behaviour and slow academic progress.

The majority of comorbid conditions in ASD are either treatable, or their impact can be significantly ameliorated through the use of specific support strategies.

Teachers' and parents' awareness of these is of paramount importance. By picking up on possible symptoms, teachers can alert parents and appropriate services such as a local educational psychologist or Child and Adolescent Mental Health Service (CAMHS) and obtain the necessary support for the pupil.

The following are some examples of the types of comorbid condition frequently seen in children with ASD.

ANXIETY DISORDERS

Anxiety disorders have been identified in research as the most frequent problem for children with ASD and they have a major impact on a child's ability to function. There are many forms of anxiety disorder. Some may be most apparent in specific situations (such as social phobia or panic disorder). In others, children are prone to be anxious most of the time, as tends to be the case for children with generalised anxiety disorder. However, it is less frequent for just one anxiety diagnosis to occur in isolation and children often develop several anxiety conditions at the same time.

How can we recognise anxiety in children with ASD?

Children with ASD may not talk openly about being worried and may find it very difficult to express their feelings even when encouraged to talk by a concerned adult. Therefore, symptoms of anxiety may often be apparent only from the child's behaviour, such as avoiding certain situations, asking repetitive questions or complaining of different aches. It is also important to highlight that many children are able to disguise their anxiety symptoms at school but may have temper tantrums and 'meltdowns' at home.

If increased anxiety is suspected, this should be discussed with the parents/carers and advice given to consult a GP regarding a possible referral to a child and adolescent psychiatrist or psychologist via CAMHS, if appropriate.

DEPRESSION

Children with ASD are also very vulnerable to developing low mood and depression. This can be due to a number of reasons, either directly associated with ASD or as a result of the increased environmental stressors for which children with ASD are often at risk, such as social isolation and bullying. Some studies have found rates of depression as high as 30% in Asperger's syndrome (e.g. Wing, 1981).

How can we recognise depression in children with ASD?

As with anxiety, pupils may not be able to express their feelings verbally or nonverbally, via facial expression or tone of voice. Consequently, the signs of depression can often be observed through behavioural changes, such as increase or decrease in appetite and sleep, decrease in activity level, increase in irritability, low motivation and self-confidence.

If depression is suspected, this should be discussed with the parents/carers. They should be advised to consult a GP regarding a possible referral to a child and adolescent psychiatrist or psychologist via CAMHS, if appropriate.

ATTENTION DEFICIT HYPERACTIVITY DISORDER (ADHD)

Children with ASD are much more likely than other children to have ADHD: research has shown that nearly a third of children with ASD have comorbid ADHD. ADHD is defined by three symptoms: hyperactivity, inattention and impulsivity. ADHD can have an immense impact on a child's functioning, especially in the school environment. Children with ADHD can frequently get into trouble as they are viewed as 'badly behaved' or disrespectful.

How can we recognise ADHD in children with ASD?

Children with ADHD present with difficulties including problems with concentration and sustained attention. They typically present with the following types of behaviour in the classroom: shouting out answers instead of putting up their hands and waiting patiently for their turn; fidgeting and squirming in their seats; being unable to follow instructions; failing to complete work or avoiding things that require a lot of effort. If ADHD is suspected, this should be discussed with the parents/carers and they should be advised to consult a GP regarding a possible referral to a child and adolescent psychiatrist or psychologist via CAMHS, if appropriate. The National Attention Deficit Disorder Information and Support Service also provides helpful information for parents and teachers: www.addiss.co.uk.

SPECIFIC LEARNING DIFFICULTIES

Although most children with ASD are of average or above-average intellectual (cognitive) ability, pupils with ASD are at increased risk of having a very uneven profile of abilities or of having specific learning difficulties (e.g. dyslexia or dyscalculia). Specific learning difficulties are characterised by the pupil's attainment in a given subject skill being significantly below the level expected based on their overall cognitive ability. Typically, a child with average or above-average cognitive ability will show particular difficulty with skills such as reading, spelling or numeracy. Therefore, if a pupil is making steady progress in a range of subjects, but is not progressing appropriately with their literacy, reading and spelling, a referral for assessment of possible dyslexia may be useful (see also Chapter 3, Language Difficulties, for a description of specific language impairment).

How can we recognise specific learning difficulties in children with ASD?

Children with ASD can have a very uneven profile of skills, with areas of real strength and unexpected difficulty. Consequently, if the pupil excels or does well in one area and struggles with another, it can sometimes be misperceived as a lack of interest or motivation, or even that the pupil is not trying hard enough. This is especially the case with less well-known difficulties, such as problems with working memory or auditory processing.

If specific learning difficulties are suspected, an educational psychologist should be consulted for a possible screening or assessment.

LEARNING DISABILITY (LD)

Although most children with ASD have average cognitive potential, the rates of learning disability in children with ASD are increased compared to the general population. Unlike specific learning difficulty, which refers to a particular area of learning (such as dyslexia), learning disability is defined as a child's overall delay in development. It is formally diagnosed if the child's overall IQ and their adaptive functioning falls at or below 70 as measured by standardised tests.

How can we recognise learning disability in children with ASD?

Identifying those children with ASD who may have a comorbid learning disability is not always straightforward. The cognitive ability of children with ASD can easily be over- or underestimated for several reasons. For example, a child's difficulties with social interaction can sometimes lead people to think they are less intelligent than they actually are. In contrast, the cognitive ability of children with ASD who use stereotyped language may be significantly overestimated, since their utterances will often sound complex and even adult-like. Unfortunately it is not unusual for a child with ASD to 'slip through the net' and fail to receive a formal diagnosis of LD. Children in this situation miss out on the appropriate educational support to which they are entitled.

If LD is suspected or a child is not performing as well as expected at school, a referral to an educational psychologist should be made with the consent of parents/carers.

DYSPRAXIA

Dyspraxia is a condition involving problems with motor planning and coordination. Children with ASD often present with a delay in acquiring motor skills, which may be apparent for both fine and gross motor skills. Difficulties with motor coordination can have a significant impact on a child's academic and even social functioning. For example, children with fine motor skills problems may have significant difficulty with writing and may consequently fail to perform to the best of their ability during exams or in lessons in general (e.g. not managing to write down the assigned homework). Sadly, research indicates that children with ASD who additionally have gross motor skills problems are at an even greater risk of bullying and social isolation than other children with ASD. Difficulties with coordination may require adaptations to be made in sports/PE classes. This can mean isolation and teasing from peers. Team sports are often the biggest challenge for a child with ASD. In some cases it can be helpful to practise skills which are difficult for the child, including catching and throwing balls, cycling and running. In some cases it is necessary to make adjustments for children with ASD who find certain parts of the PE class too demanding and challenging due to their condition. It can be a much better idea to get children with ASD doing activities and sports that are more suited to them. Swimming can help, as can sports that do not have an emphasis on teamwork but allow individuals to perform at their own pace (e.g. running, golf, trampoline, karate or self-defence).

How can we recognise dyspraxia in children with ASD?

Children with dyspraxia often appear clumsy. Their difficulties with gross motor skills may be apparent during PE, but will also be noticeable in their day-to-day functioning. They will often be more likely than their peers to bump into or break things. Fine motor difficulties are reflected in messy and slow handwriting. Further information and support is available from the Dyspraxia Foundation (http://www. dyspraxiafoundation.org.uk/index.php).

OBSESSIVE-COMPULSIVE DISORDER (OCD)

Obsessive-compulsive disorder is a form of anxiety disorder characterised by recurrent obsessional thoughts or compulsive acts. Obsessional thoughts are ideas that enter the child's mind. They are usually distressing and the child may try to resist them.

Common obsessions are, for example, a fear of germs. Compulsions are behaviours that are repeated again and again. A common example is handwashing. OCD tends to be associated with significant distress, such as an extreme fear that something bad will happen if they do not perform the ritual.

How can we recognise OCD in children with ASD?

It can sometimes be difficult to distinguish obsessions and compulsions from the core symptoms of ASD (e.g. the obsessions, routines and rituals often seen in ASD). OCD can often go unrecognised for long periods of time as children with OCD often hide their symptoms due to being embarrassed and feeling scared that they are 'going crazy'.

Children may sometimes behave in unusual ways, for example, being late for school (due to checking repeatedly, e.g. that all the switches are turned off, or that the door is locked) even if it's not in their nature to be late. Parents might often have more opportunities to observe such symptoms. If OCD is suspected or reported by parents, they should be advised to consult a GP regarding a possible referral to a child and adolescent psychiatrist or psychologist via CAMHS, if appropriate.

TOURETTE/TIC SYNDROME

Tourette syndrome is a condition characterised by motor and vocal tics (involuntary movements or noises). Perhaps one of the most well-known forms of vocal tics is coprolalia (inappropriate and involuntary swearing), this however only affects a very small proportion of children. Much more common vocal tics are: throat clearing, sniffing, repeating the last word that they or someone else has said. Tourette syndrome is around two to three times more common in people with autism than in the general population. It can be distressing for the child and can lead to teasing or bullying. The tics can also sometimes get children into trouble at school if people mistakenly think they have control over the behaviour. Furthermore, children with Tourette syndrome can often devote a lot of energy and concentration to suppressing their tics in the classroom. This affects their ability to pay full attention during class.

The condition can be treated with psychological strategies and/or medication so if any form of tics is observed it is very helpful to consult a GP regarding a possible referral to a child and adolescent psychiatrist or psychologist via CAMHS, if appropriate.

FEEDING AND EATING PROBLEMS

Feeding problems are more common in children with ASD. A common presentation is where the child with ASD eats a restricted range of foods or only eat foods of a particular colour or texture. The child may also have certain rituals around eating which can limit the food intake (e.g. eating food in a particular order). Research indicates that children with ASD may also have a somewhat increased incidence of eating disorders, such as anorexia nervosa.

Restrictions and rituals around food become of concern if the child is not taking in the range of nutrients they require to grow, or if their weight and/or height are not increasing as expected. If there are concerns about feeding and eating problems, parents should be advised to consult a GP regarding a possible referral to a paediatrician, child and adolescent psychiatrist or psychologist via CAMHS, if appropriate.

EPILEPSY

ASD is also associated with a higher incidence of epilepsy but it is hoped that by the time a child has reached secondary school this condition would have been recognised and treated by a specialist (e.g. a paediatric neurologist). Seizures, caused by abnormal electrical activity in the brain, can produce a temporary loss of consciousness, body convulsions, unusual movements, or absent episodes. There is a risk of longer-term damage to the brain if seizures are prolonged. If such difficulties are suspected, therefore, parents/carers should be advised to contact a GP as soon as possible.

 ## FINAL CONSIDERATIONS

Children with ASD are often likely to have additional developmental problems, such as ADHD, or mental health and emotional difficulties, such as anxiety, depression or conduct problems. The effects of these may be underestimated and can impact a great deal on the child academically and emotionally, ultimately resulting in challenging behaviour being exhibited in school. By being aware of a child's comorbid difficulties and the support strategies available, education staff can help to improve the child's functioning and wellbeing at school. If teaching staff become aware of additional problems it is important to alert the parents/carers and the appropriate services such as a local educational psychologist or Child and Adolescent Mental Health Service.

BIBLIOGRAPHY

Attwood, T. (2004). *Exploring feelings: Cognitive behaviour therapy to manage anxiety*. Arlington, TX: Future Horizons.

Baker, J. (2003). *Social Skills Training for Children and Adolescents with Asperger Syndrome and Social-Communications Problems*. Shawnee Mission, KS: Autism Asperger Publishing Co.

Barrett, W., & Randall, L. (2004). Investigating the circle of friends approach: Adaptations and implications for practice. *Educational Psychology in Practice*, 20(4), 353–368.

Buzan, T (2002). *How to Mind Map: The ultimate thinking tool that will change your life*. London: Thorsons.

Carter, C., Meckes, L., Pritchard, L., Swensen, S., Wittman, P. P., & Velde, B. (2004). The friendship club: An after-school program for children with Asperger Syndrome. *Family and Community Health*, 27, 143–150.

Frankel, F., & Myatt, R. (2003). Children's friendship training. New York: Brunner-Routledge Publishers.

Frederickson, N., Warren, L., & Turner, J. (2005). 'Circle of friends' – An exploration of impact over time. *Educational Psychology in Practice*, 21(3), 197–21.

Garrison-Harrell, L., Kamps, D., Kravits, T. (1997). The effects of peer networks on social-communicative behaviors for students with autism. *Focus on Autism and Other Developmental Disabilities*, 12(4), 241–254.

Gillot, A., Furniss, F., & Walter, A. (2001). Anxiety in high-functioning children with autism. *Autism*, 5(3), 277–286.

Gray, C. (1994). *Comic Strip Conversations: Illustrated interactions that teach conversation skills to students with autism and related disorders*. Arlington, TX: Future Horizons.

Gray, C. (2000). *The new Social Story book: Illustrated edition*. Arlington, TX: Future Horizons.

Gray, C. (2010). *The new Social Story book*. Arlington, TX: Future Horizons.

House of Commons Education Committee (2011). Behaviour and Discipline in Schools [White paper]. Retrieved from http://www.publications.parliament.uk/pa/cm201011/cmselect/cmeduc/516/51602.htm

Gus, L. (2000). Autism: Promoting peer understanding. *Educational Psychology in Practice*, 16(3), 461–468.

Kalyva, E., & Avramidis, E. (2005). Improving communication between children with autism and their peers through the 'Circle of Friends': A small-scale intervention study. *Journal of Applied Research in Intellectual Disabilities*, 18, 253–261.

Kanner, L. (1943). Autistic disturbances of affective contact. *Nervous Child*, 2, 217–250.

Kluth, P., & Schwarz, P. (2008). *Just give him the whale*. Baltimore: Paul H. Brookes Publishing.

Laugeson, E., & Frankel, F. (2010). *Social skills for teenagers with developmental and autism spectrum disorders. The PEERS treatment manual*. New York: Routledge.

Marr, N., & Field, T. (2001). *Bully side: Death at playtime*. Oxford: Wessex Press.

Program for the Education and Enrichment of Relational Skills (PEERS) Teaching autistic teens to make friends/ Available at http://www.semel.ucla.edu/peers/news/09/apr/07/teaching-autistic-teens-make-friends

Smith, C. (2003). *Writing and Developing Social Stories: Practical Interventions*. Telford: Speechmark.

Stallard, P. (2005). *A clinician's guide to think good–feel good: Using CBT with children and young people*. Chichester: John Wiley & Sons.

Stobart, A. (2009) *Bullying and autism spectrum disorders: a guide for school staff* (booklet: can be purchased from the National Autistic Society website http://www.autism.org.uk/products/core-nas-publications/bullying-and-asd.aspx).

Taylor, G. (1997). Community building in schools: Developing a circle of friends. *Educational and Child Psychology*, 14(3), 45–50.

Welton, J., & Telford, J. (2004). *What did you say? What do you mean?: An illustrated guide to understanding metaphors.* London: Jessica Kingsley Publishers.

Whitaker, P. (2001). *Challenging behaviour and autism: Making sense, making progress.* London: The National Autistic Society.

Wing, L. (1981). Asperger's syndrome: A clinical account. *Psychological Medicine*, 11, 115–119.

Ylvisaker, M., & Feeney, T. (2002). Executive functions, self regulation, and learned optimism in pediatric rehabilitation: a review and implications for intervention. *Pediatric Rehabilitation*, 1–20.

Zarkowska, E., & Clements, J. (1994). *Care staff management: A practitioner's guide.* Oxford: John Wiley & Sons.

PART THREE

APPENDICES

APPENDIX 1

Adult Screening Questionnaire

This Screening Questionnaire is designed in such a way as to enable school professionals and parents/carers to evaluate the child's difficulties on a scale of significance.
Name of person completing this form:
Relationship to child:
Pupil's name:
Pupil's date of birth:
Pupil's diagnosed conditions: (please list all diagnoses, such as ASD, dyspraxia, dyslexia, ADHD, etc.)
Is pupil aware of diagnosis: ASD: ☐ Yes   ☐ No Any other diagnoses: ☐ Yes   ☐ No
Does the pupil and family consent to the diagnosis being shared with: Staff: ☐ Yes   ☐ No Peers: ☐ Yes   ☐ No
Does pupil have Statement of Special Educational Needs: ☐ Yes   ☐ No If yes, please list below the sessions for which the pupil receives 1:1 support (e.g. PE, group work):
Critical medical needs: (conditions requiring medication or special considerations, such as diabetes, allergies, etc.)

Please tick the support needs which apply to the pupil on the scale below, according to relevant level of significance:

1 – indicates that it is an area school professionals need to be aware of

2 – indicates that it is an area which will require specific support strategies

3 – indicates a priority area which will require a proactive and consistent management plan

Please indicate the child's areas of difficulty by ticking the appropriate boxes below.

Question/statements	Level of significance		
Social Interaction Difficulties			
	1	2	3
Has he/she had difficulty making friends in the past?			
Has he/she had difficulty in sustaining friendships?			
Has he/she been worried about making friends?			
Does he/she have difficulty joining conversations?			
Does he/she have difficulty with turn-taking during a game or other activity?			
Does he/she have difficulty cooperating with others in the classroom or during sporting activities?			
Does he/she have difficulty understanding indirect hints or cues in conversation? (e.g. that someone yawning might mean that they are bored)			
Was he/she socially isolated from peers at primary school?			
Does he/she have difficulty making appropriate use of nonverbal communication? (e.g. too little or too much of any the following: gesture, eye contact or facial expression)			
Any other areas of concern:			
Thinking about this area, have any strategies proved successful in the past?			

cont.

1 – indicates that it is an area school professionals need to be aware of
2 – indicates that it is an area which will require specific support strategies
3 – indicates a priority area which will require a proactive and consistent management plan

Language Difficulties

	1	2	3
Does he/she have difficulty following longer directions given by the teacher? (e.g. only following the last step of a three-step sequence)			
Do you notice that he/she misinterprets what has been said or needs things repeated?			
Does he/she make grammatical errors when speaking?			
Do you notice that he/she has difficulty naming items?			
Do you notice that he/she sometimes interprets figures of speech literally? (e.g. 'pull your socks up')			

Any other areas of concern:

Thinking about this area, have any strategies proved successful in the past?

Difficulties with Imagination and Flexible Thinking

	1	2	3
Does he/she have difficulty with change? (e.g. changing activities, rooms, or routine)			
Does he/she have difficulties with flexibility? (e.g. difficulty with creative problem solving, shifting between tasks or changing topic)			
Does he/she have intense interests or preoccupations, which affect his/her social interaction?			
Does he/she have any compulsions? (e.g. insistence on completing a task, careful placement of things, checking and becoming anxious if these activities are disrupted)			
Does he/she display insistence on rituals or routines that if not completed would lead to anxiety?			

Any other areas of concern:

Thinking about this area, have any strategies proved successful in the past?

Bullying

	1	2	3
Has he/she experienced bullying in the past?			
Is he/she vulnerable to being bullied?			
Would you describe him/her as being a loner, hence more vulnerable?			
Does he/she misinterpret social cues and hence could be seen as an 'easy target'?			
Is he/she overly keen to please and hence vulnerable to exploitation?			
Does he/she have difficulty distinguishing teasing/bullying from non-deliberate events?			
Is he/she at risk of being perceived as a bully due to being literal or prone to telling people what to do?			
Is he/she prone to responding with challenging behaviour due to difficulty using language?			
Are there specific behaviours which make him/her particularly vulnerable to being bullied? (e.g. talking to him/herself, difficulties with getting dressed after PE, etc.). If yes, please list below:			

cont.

Any other areas of concern:

Thinking about this area, have any strategies proved successful in the past?

1 – indicates that it is an area school professionals need to be aware of

2 – indicates that it is an area which will require specific support strategies

3 – indicates a priority area which will require a proactive and consistent management plan

Planning and Organisation Problems

Compared to other children in his/her class does the child have significant difficulty with:

	1	2	3
Planning? (e.g. starts projects without having a plan/begins a task and then does not know what to do next/struggles with large assignments)			
Flexibility? (e.g. finds it difficult moving from one activity to another/struggles at transition points during the day/persists with an approach to a task even when it is not working)			
Initiation? (e.g. has trouble coming up with new ideas/always needs prompting to get started with schoolwork/when given a new task 'just sits there')			
Organisation? (e.g. written work is poorly structured/regularly arrives at lessons without necessary materials/looses things all the time)			
Short-term memory? (e.g. has a short attention span/forgets task instructions involving more than two steps/forgets what he/she is supposed to be doing)			

Any other areas of concern:

Thinking about this area, have any strategies proved successful in the past?

Sensory Sensitivities

	1	2	3
Do you notice that he/she has visual sensory issues? (e.g. dislikes bright lights, is fascinated by shiny objects and bright colours, enjoys certain patterns such as brickwork, stripes)			
Do you notice that he/she has sensory issues related to noise and sound? (e.g. finds crowded areas very difficult, covers ears in response to certain sounds, can hear sounds which others do not hear, enjoys certain sounds like banging objects and doors)			
Do you notice that he/she has sensory issues related to smell or taste? (e.g. smelling or licking items/people, or has strong dislike for certain everyday smells)			
Do you notice that he/she has sensory issues related to touch and feel? (e.g. dislikes the feel of certain fabrics and substances, seems unaware of pain and temperature, dislikes crunchy or chewy food)			

Any other areas of concern:

Thinking about this area, have any strategies proved successful in the past?

cont.

1 – indicates that it is an area school professionals need to be aware of
2 – indicates that it is an area which will require specific support strategies
3 – indicates a priority area which will require a proactive and consistent management plan

Anxiety/Worries

	1	2	3
Is he/she very anxious about the transition to secondary school?			
Is he/she generally shy, withdrawn or anxious?			
Is he/she very anxious when meeting new people?			
Is he/she worried about academic work and pressure?			
Is he/she worried when faced with changes in routine?			

Are there other specific worries he/she has in relation to school? (e.g. PE, detention, homework, getting lost, toilets). Please list below:

Any other areas of concern:

Thinking about this area, have any strategies proved successful in the past?

Challenging Behaviour			
	1	2	3
Does he/she frequently interrupt class by, for example, asking repetitive questions?			
Does he/she say rude or inappropriate things in class?			
Does he/she defend himself/herself physically by hitting other children?			
Does he/she have difficulty following classroom or school rules?			
Does he/she have difficulty controlling angry or hurt feelings when he/she does not get his/her own way?			

Any other areas of concern:

Thinking about this area, have any strategies proved successful in the past?

Child Screening Questionnaire

This should be completed by the child with help from parents/carers before the Bridge Meeting. The child should use his/her own words.

My name is: . . . .

My date of birth is:. . . . .

What are three thing you *are not* looking forward to about moving to secondary school?

1.
2.
3.

What are three thing you *are* looking forward to about moving to secondary school?

1.
2.
3.

Here are some things about moving to secondary school that children have said they might feel worried about. Please put a *circle* around the symbol that shows how you feel about each of these things.

	No worries	Worried	Not sure
Big playground/school/ getting around	☺	☹	?
Getting into trouble	☺	☹	?
New teachers	☺	☹	?
Clothes/uniform	☺	☹	?
Making friends	☺	☹	?
Schoolwork/homework	☺	☹	?
Sports and activities	☺	☹	?

cont.

	No worries	Worried	Not sure
Bullying	🙂	☹️	❓
Computers/technology/equipment/new lessons	🙂	☹️	❓
New food	🙂	☹️	❓
Going on public transport/getting to school	🙂	☹️	❓
Library/reading	🙂	☹️	❓

Transition Management Plan

To be circulated to everyone at Bridge Meeting and a copy to kept with the child's file & with SENCO

During the Bridge Meeting parents/carers and professionals agreed on the following plan for transition to secondary school:

Transition plan for (name of child):
Name of primary school:
Name of secondary school:
Primary school main contact:
Secondary school main contact:

General Transition Strategies

Delete as appropriate	Agreed dates	Relevant information
Visiting the school		
Maps or layout of school		
Photos of school rooms/ buildings		
Photos of school staff		
Allocated staff member identified		
Copy of school rules		
Copy of school timetable		
Any other strategies		

SPECIFIC TRANSITION STRATEGIES EXAMPLE

Specific Transition Strategies

Area of support	Details (reasons)	Strategies/ resources	Notes	Person responsible	When
Priority 1 Social interaction	Child is eager to have friends but struggles to initiate friendships	Chapter 2, Social Interaction in Transition Pack, Identifying a buddy, Structured lunch time activity with a child who has similar interests	Primary teacher suggests David, a friend from primary school	Mrs McCain, SENCO in secondary school	To be set up first term of secondary school
Priority 2 Challenging behaviour	Challenging behaviour when there is a change in routine	Chapter 9, Challenging Behaviour in pack			
Priority 3					
Priority					
Priority					

Additional concerns for staff to be aware of:

Known motivators/interests: (e.g. music facts)

Triggers/dislikes: (e.g. group work)

Calming techniques:

SPECIFIC TRANSITION STRATEGIES

Specific Transition Strategies

Area of support	Details (reasons)	Strategies/ resources	Notes	Person responsible	When
Priority 1					
Priority 2					
Priority 3					
Priority					
Priority					

Additional concerns for staff to be aware of:

Known motivators/interests: (e.g. music facts)

Triggers/dislikes: (e.g. group work)

Calming techniques:

APPENDIX 4

Pupil Profile

To be circulated to ALL school staff in secondary school and a copy to kept with child's file & with SENCO

Insert pupil's photograph	Name of pupil:	DOB:
	Class:	Form tutor/ allocated support staff:

Pupil's diagnosed conditions: (please list all diagnoses, such as ASD, dyspraxia, dyslexia, ADHD, etc.)

Is pupil aware of diagnosis?:
ASD: ☐ Yes ☐ No

Any other diagnoses: ☐ Yes ☐ No

Does the pupil and family consent to the diagnosis being shared with others?
Staff: ☐ Yes ☐ No

Peers: ☐ Yes ☐ No

Does pupil have Statement of Special Educational Needs? ☐ Yes ☐ No

If yes, please list below the sessions for which the pupil receives 1:1 support: (e.g. PE, group work)

Critical medical needs: (conditions requiring medication or special considerations, such as diabetes, allergies, etc.)

Areas of strength/positive attributes:

Area of support need (1):

Agreed support strategies (1):

Area of support need (2):

Agreed support strategies (2):

Area of support need (3):

Agreed support strategies (3):

Does pupil have any specific requirements (such as extra time during exams, or use of specific technology to help with difficulties with handwriting, etc.)?

Homework support: (e.g. homework club)	Class modifications: (e.g. sits at single desk)

Additional concerns of which staff need to be aware:

Known motivators/interests: (e.g. music facts)

Triggers/dislikes: (e.g. group work)

Calming techniques:

How Does the Triad of Impairments Present in the Classroom?

(From Part 1 of the pack, Creating an Individualised Transition Plan)

What follows are examples of how behaviours or difficulties associated with ASD present in the classroom.

DIFFICULTIES WITH SOCIAL COMMUNICATION

Area of difficulty	Implications in the classroom
Difficulty with interpreting nonverbal communication	Nonverbal communication is essential for understanding the meaning of verbal information. Each statement can have a totally contradictory meaning, depending on the tone of voice, facial expression or the gestures we use. *Example: Mark, a pupil in the classroom, becomes angry with his classmate Luke, who has ASD and tends to talk to himself. Using a warning tone of voice, gesture and facial expression, Mark threatens: 'Say that once again, and...' So Luke repeats it, as Mark asked him to. Mark gets even more upset, and the teacher intervenes: 'Luke, why did you repeat that, when Mark asked you not to?' Genuinely confused, Luke pleads: 'But he asked me to say it again...'*
Precise understanding of language	It is difficult to appreciate how imprecise our communication is and how heavily we rely on the ability of the listener to understand our communicative intent. *Example: A well-known speaker who has ASD kindly gives talks to professionals about its impact on social interaction. She presented at a conference on the topic of the difficulties with precise understanding of language. At the end of her talk, she invites questions. One member of the audience politely asks: 'Can I ask you a question...?' She answers 'Yes' and turns to the audience: 'Any other questions?'*
Literal interpretation of the language	Children with ASD often have difficulty with understanding figurative use of language, metaphors or even common sayings. *Example: Luke, a pupil with ASD, is reluctant to attempt a task for a long time, and despite his teacher's patience and encouragement, he keeps procrastinating and becomes anxious. The teacher says: 'Luke, pull your socks up!' Luke proceeds to pull both of his socks up and the whole class gasps at his inappropriate reaction to a teacher, who was trying to be kind to him, whilst Luke is pleased with himself for doing what was asked of him...*

Difficulties with making conversation/'small talk'	In conversation, children tend to spontaneously elaborate on their responses in order to sustain the conversation. Some children with ASD can have extreme difficulties in this area.
	Example: Mark tries to be friendly towards Luke, a peer with ASD, and asks: 'Do you have any pets?' 'Yes', Luke answers. Mark waits for him to tell him about his pets, but since Mark didn't say anything, Luke asks: 'What pets do you have?' 'A dog', Luke answers. Mark waits for Luke to tell him about his dog, but after a moment of silence he asks 'That's lovely, what is your dog like? 'Good', Luke answers. Mark leaves disappointed thinking that Luke does not want to make friends with him. Luke is devastated that Mark left, and does not understand why, as he thought he answered all of his questions, not realising Mark expected him to elaborate on these...
Difficulties with reciprocal conversation	Even children with an advanced level of vocabulary for their age may not have the skills to pick up on conversational 'cliff-hangers' intended to invite a question in return, or may not know how to relinquish conversational turns.
	Example: Luke, a pupil with ASD, keeps talking about his favourite computer game. His peer, Mark, listens to him patiently and, excited that he has a common interest with Luke, says: 'I have a favourite game, too!' Luke continues 'In my game...' Mark is left thinking what a self-centred boy Luke is, not realising that he does not know how to relinquish conversational turns or ask for further information...
Difficulties with following the sequences of instructions and difficulties with describing sequences of events	Although children with ASD may not have obvious difficulties with language, they may still find it extremely difficult to follow a sequence of instructions, or to describe a sequence of events. This can be a source of significant frustration not only for the child, but also for the teachers, unless they have available strategies to help them.
	Example: After a history lesson, during which Luke, a pupil with ASD, was able to provide the most detailed information about the Roman Empire, a conflict arose between Luke and Mark. The teacher thoughtfully intervenes, trying to help them resolve the issue. Mark describes exactly what upset him. Luke just keeps repeating: 'It wasn't fair,' but is unable to describe what he perceives to be unfair. As the teacher has only one account of the event, and as it would be difficult to imagine that a child who has just been able to relay the most complex information they have learned by rote is not able to describe a simple sequence of events, the teacher has no choice but to assume that Luke does not want to explain what happened, because he is in the wrong...
Using language in an overly formal way	Many children with ASD may have an excellent memory for long words and phrases. They may repeat whole chunks of expressions they have learnt from adults, movies or books without realising that this may not be appropriate in the given context or that this may appear patronising.
	Example: Luke, a secondary pupil with ASD, trying to contribute to the discussion about the importance of reading: 'Education has produced a vast population able to read but unable to distinguish what is worth reading.' The whole class feels upset, feeling that he was patronising about their choice of books, not realising that he merely repeated a well-known quotation by a famous British historian, G. M. Trevelyan, without understanding the impact it would have on others...

DIFFICULTIES WITH SOCIAL INTERACTION

Area of difficulty	Implications in the classroom
Difficulty with eye contact	Some children may have a difficulty with modulating their eye contact appropriately to the social situation. The child may either avoid eye contact, or their eye contact can appear too intense. *Example 1: Luke, a pupil with ASD, is taught during the social skills group that eye contact is important in order to make people feel they are being listened to. Luke asks: 'But I can either look or listen. Should I look at them even if that means I will get distracted and not be able to listen to them properly?'* *Example 2: Luke, a pupil with ASD, is taught during the social skills group that eye contact is important. He then gets into trouble with the older peers, who accuse him of staring at them.*
Difficulty with identifying and expressing emotions verbally or nonverbally	Most children with ASD have significant difficulties with identifying and expressing their emotions verbally or nonverbally. This means that the child may have the same facial expression, often the same 'fixed smile', even when they are confused or distressed. This can make it very difficult for the teachers to 'read' the pupil and know how to help them. *Example: The teacher is explaining new material. Luke, a pupil with ASD, sits peacefully, and appears to listen. He is smiling. The teacher checks with everyone if they have understood the information, but Luke does not say anything and does not look confused. So the teacher continues, pleased that everyone has understood. However, Luke missed more than 60% of the instructions, which by now has left him feeling utterly frustrated. When the teacher finalises the instructions and asks the pupils to work independently, Luke's frustration reaches its peak, as he is utterly lost, and he has a 'meltdown'. The teacher is understandably confused about Luke's unexpected reaction, as they have double-checked with everyone at every step, whilst Luke's frustration grew to the point where he was no longer able to control it. He was not given any specific instructions to put his hand or card up when he was confused, so he did not realise that he should have done so...*
Difficulty with making friends	Children with ASD tend to have significant difficulty making friends. They may not know how to approach other children, or how to play in cooperative ways. As a result, children with ASD have been perceived to be loners. However, whilst a few children are happy in their own company, most children with ASD are very keen to make friends and be accepted. *Example: Luke, a pupil with ASD, keeps watching other children play in the playground. He never goes up to them, but he appears happy, so no one interferes. However, Luke is desperate to join them, but just does not know how to. One day, he comes home from school so upset that he is determined not to go back, because 'no one likes him'. When his parents and teachers probe further, trying to encourage him to return, they learn that he has been hoping to be included in games for two terms, but no one asked him to join their group. Both his parents and teachers feel at a loss, as Luke has never expressed his wish to be included before.*

Difficulty with insight into different social situations and sustaining friendships	A lot of children with ASD have a difficulty with social reciprocity, sharing and basic skills necessary for collaborating with others in a cooperative manner. *Example: Luke, a boy with ASD, was working with a group of children with whom he was friendly. He was very keen for his group to do particularly well, and hence he was telling other children what to do, not realising that this would upset them and make them feel he was not listening to their views.*
Difficulties picking up on social clues	Understanding of the social context is essential in order to ensure that our behaviour is appropriate to the circumstances. However, as most children with ASD are unable to take this into consideration, even their well-meant comments or actions can appear to be highly inappropriate. *Example: A teacher explains to a group of children that they should not be doing something. Luke, a boy with ASD, who is very keen to do well and has been taught that 'the teacher is always right', consequently reprimands the children for doing the same thing later on. Whilst Luke meant well, he did not realise that the same words coming from him will not be perceived in the same way as when a teacher says them, as the social context has changed.*
Vulnerability to exploitation/ teasing	Children with ASD tend to have a significant difficulty with understanding people's intentions. As many children with ASD are so keen to fit in and please, they are very vulnerable to teasing or exploitation, without being able to realise the consequences of their actions. *Example: Children were teasing Luke, a boy with ASD, and told him that it is really cool to take sweets from the shop and if he does it, he will become popular. As Luke was extremely keen to fit in, he followed their 'advice' and consequently got into trouble.*

DIFFICULTIES WITH IMAGINATION AND FLEXIBLE THINKING

Area of difficulty	Implications in the classroom
Difficulties adjusting to change	Children with ASD often find change very difficult. Even minor changes, which are sometimes difficult to avoid, can be very unsettling for them. *Example: Times when a schedule has to change, for example, due to the teacher's unexpected absence, can be very distressing for children with ASD, and they may need a more thorough explanation and support to be able to cope than their peers.*

cont.

Area of difficulty	Implications in the classroom
Intense interests and preoccupations	Many children with ASD have strong, preoccupying interests. Pupils' fixations may sometimes interfere with their ability to be able to focus on other aspects of the curriculum or may even interfere with social interaction and other activities. *Example: Luke, a pupil with ASD, had a preoccupying interest in computers, to the extent that he found it difficult to dedicate his attention to other subjects. He was falling significantly behind in reading and writing and his peers were finding his constant talk about computers increasingly difficult. Utilising his strong interests to help him to work on his areas of difficulty (for example assigning Luke to do extra reading or writing about a particular aspect of computers), and scheduling a special 'computer time' for him on a daily basis as a reward for focusing on other areas of curriculum, has helped him to make the most of his abilities. Furthermore, setting up a reciprocal arrangement during which Luke helped other children with IT helped him to develop social skills and friendships.*
Adherence to specific routines/need for things to be done in a specific way	Although this may not apply to all pupils with ASD, for those to whom it does, this area can be a challenge and can cause great distress. *Example: Luke, a boy with ASD, could eat his food only when it was separated, so that no textures would mix. Carrying his food on a tray to a table in the canteen, he tilted his plate so that the sauce touched his potatoes. Luke was not able to eat his food because he can only eat his food if it is separated. Luke approached the canteen worker, complaining that his sauce was touching his potatoes and asked for a new plate of food. Without having a specific understanding of his difficulties, staff would be inclined to think that he needs to 'learn to eat his food' and send him back. This resulted in Luke being distressed and hungry for the rest of the day.*
Compulsive tendencies	Some pupils with ASD have a strong, compulsive need to do or complete certain things in a certain way, which may interfere with other activities. *Example: When Luke, a boy with ASD, was asked a question, he had to complete the whole list of points in his answers and would become very distressed if interrupted. His friend, who also has ASD, had a strong need to prepare all of his materials on his desk when he arrived for class, before he could do anything else, including saying 'hello' to others. Both reactions could be perceived as unfriendly, unless others understood the reasons behind them.*
Sensory sensitivities	This difficulty may not apply to all children, but it can cause significant impairment. So many children with ASD seem to have a significant issue with sensory over/under-sensitivity that many research studies argue more attention should be paid to this area. *Example: Some children may be over-sensitive to visual, auditory or tactile stimulation. The material of the school uniform, or the background noises or lights in a classroom may be preoccupying to such an extent that the pupil may have only a very limited ability to pay attention to other, often crucial elements of information.*

APPENDIX 6

Turn-Taking

(Referred to in Chapter 2, Social Interaction)

What is it for?	To promote social inclusion
Who is it for?	Should be practised with an adult (teacher, SENCO, parent/carer)
How is it to be used?	Show cartoon and explain rules to child. Use visual cue cards to prompt turn-taking behaviour in classroom setting.
When is it to be used?	To be introduced and practised in designated quiet time or social skills group

TURN-TAKING RULES

We try to take turns when we talk with someone.

1.
This boy talks   This boy listens

2.
Now this boy listens   This boy talks

3.
Now this boy talks   This boy listens

4.
Now this boy listens   This boy talks

VISUAL CUE CARDS

Show this picture whenever you are talking about taking turns.

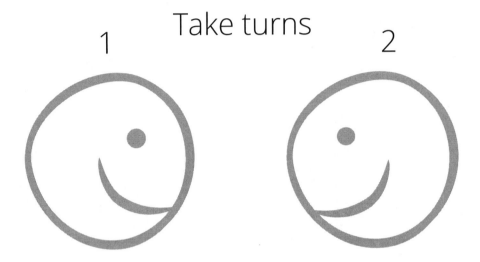

Source: Adapted from Pelican Talk: www.pelicantalk.com

APPENDIX 7

Rules in Conversation and Rules when Entering a Group

(Referred to in Chapter 2, Social Interaction)

What is it for?	To promote social skills and integration
Who is it for?	Should be practised with an adult (teacher, SENCO, parent/carer)
How is it to be used?	Show rules and explain them to child
When is it to be used?	To be introduced and practised in designated quiet time or social skills group

Rules in conversation

WHEN

When is it a GOOD time? In the breaks – between lessons or at lunch; between activities or before activities start, when someone appears lonely or bored

When is it a BAD time? When others are busy or in a rush; when others are in a deep conversation; teacher is talking/giving instructions; children are working quietly; someone else is talking/sharing their ideas – it is important to be a good listener

WHERE

Where is a GOOD place? On the playground, in the canteen, in a queue; on school grounds before or after school

Where is a BAD place? In the classroom during the lesson or work time; during a PE lesson; in a crowded hallway

HOW

What to do: Be an active listener – pay attention to what the other person is saying; find out what they are interested in; ask open-ended questions (answers that require more than yes or no for example *what have you been up to this weekend? Or, what did you think of that new video game XYZ talked about?*; think about a good time to end a conversation (all conversations eventually need to come to an end) – for example wait until the other person stops talking.

What NOT to do: take over the conversation – instead take turns; ask too many questions (you don't want to interview the other person); talk about your interests only

What worked BEST for you? (Try the rules above and write down what worked best for you.)

Rules for approaching others

WHEN

When is it a GOOD time? When someone appears lonely or bored, at a playground, after school; during a break in a game or activity

When is it a BAD time? When others are busy or in a rush; when they are engaged in a deep conversation or when everyone is expected to work quietly

WHERE

Where is a GOOD place? On the playground; on school grounds before or after school

Where is a BAD place? In the classroom; during a P E lesson; in a crowded hallway when everyone is rushing somewhere

HOW

What to do: Check out what others are doing and then choose a group you have similar interests with and would like to play with; make eye contact and wait for a pause in the game or conversation; decide what you want to say – *Can I join in?*

What NOT to do: Come and tell others what to do or not to do, correct others, tell them something that might be true, but is considered impolite or too personal, stand too close to others, or do something silly to get attention like breaking something

What worked BEST for you? (Try the rules above and write down what worked best for you.)

FURTHER READING

Frankel, F. & Myatt, R. (2003). *Children's friendship training.* New York: Brunner-Routledge Publishers. These ideas have been adapted from the PEERS programme developed at UCLA to increase social skills in teenagers.

APPENDIX 8

Carol Gray's Social Stories™

(Referred to in Chapter 2, Social Interaction)

What is it for?	To help children with ASD learn social and communication skills
Who is it for?	Should be practised with an adult (teacher, SENCO, parent/carer)
How is it to be used?	Show the Social Story and explain it to the child using the guidance included
When is it to be used?	To be introduced and practised in designated quiet time or social skills group

WHAT ARE SOCIAL STORIES™?

- Social Stories™ are a written sequence of events aimed at teaching your child how to behave in a specific circumstance. Some Social Stories™ can be represented as a comic strip with pictures if your child is not yet reading or prefers pictures.

- The idea behind Social Stories™ is to give your child a clear guideline of what happens in a particular social setting (e.g. 'What happens when my friend comes to my house' or 'How do I say hello to my teacher?' or 'What will I do when someone is not listening to me?'). You can then review these stories on a regular basis with your child so that he/she learns to internalise the behaviours and carry them out successfully.

- There are books available with ready-made Social Stories™, such as 'The New Social Story Book' (Gray 2010).

- You can write new Social Stories for any specific eventuality that arises. Some of the situations will be specific to your child. You may feel confident to write Social Stories yourself once you have reviewed Carol Gray's book. If not, 'Writing and Developing Social Stories: Practical Interventions' may be helpful (Smith, 2003).

- Use a very concrete, logical stepped approach in the story. All stories must have a beginning, middle and end: first set the scene, then identify some of the potential situations that might arise and end by giving the behaviour that you wish your child to carry out.

- All stories must be written in the 'I' form so that when your child reviews the story he/she reads it (or follows the comic strip) saying, 'I will try to…' etc. In this way it will be more real to your child.

- All stories must be written in a positive, reassuring tone.

- Do not use sweeping statements, instead use terms such as 'usually', 'often'.

- Identify the behaviour you wish your child to carry out by saying: 'I will try to... (say hello to my teacher every morning)' or 'I will try not to (get upset if someone touches my arm…)'.

- Pick a suitable title and phrase it as a question (e.g. What happens at…?/Why do people sometimes…?).

- Try to use the phrase: 'This is OK' when talking about other people's reactions.

- Try to keep all the stories in a folder and categorise them logically. Some children might prefer to keep them on computer.

EXAMPLE OF A SOCIAL STORY™

Making Mistakes

It is OK to make a mistake. When I am working on my own I might make a mistake. Everyone makes mistakes.
I can go back and correct my mistakes.
That is how I learn. Other people also learn from their mistakes.

FURTHER READING

Gray, C. (2010). *The New Social Story Book*. Arlington, TX: Future Horizons.
Smith, C. (2003). *Writing and developing Social Stories: Practical interventions*. Telford: Speechmark.

APPENDIX 9

Circle of Friends

(Referred to in Chapter 2, Social Interaction)

What is it for?	To promote social inclusion
Who is it for?	The Circle of Friends group should be facilitated by an experienced professional (e.g. educational psychologist or SENCO) in regards to issues such as confidentiality, safety and benefits for the child with ASD. In many local authorities the Autism Outreach Team provides this service.
How is it to be used?	Establish a circle of six to eight children with an adult facilitator to work collaboratively to think of ways to improve the focus child's peer relationships. Please find detailed instructions below.
When is it to be used?	To be introduced if the child is noted to feel lonely and isolated.

AIMS

The Circle of Friends intervention is a peer-based approach developed to promote the inclusion into mainstream school of students with disabilities and difficulties. This can often be used to assist children with ASD to develop their social and communication skills by engaging in the school community and peer groups. The Circle of Friends is not an approach to provide instant friendship.

THE CIRCLE OF FRIENDS WORKS AS A TEAM TO...

- Encourage the development of a support network for the child within a structured setting

- Possibly help the focus child to build closer and better relationships

- Provide encouragement and recognition for achievements and progress

- Identify difficulties the focus child faces and devise practical ideas to help deal with these difficulties.

Volunteers in the group can also benefit from increased self-esteem and social integration.

HOW TO SET UP A CIRCLE OF FRIENDS

- School discusses Circle of Friends approach with parents/carers of the focus child and obtains consent.

- Discuss with parents/carers whether or not the child is aware of the diagnosis of ASD. Circle of Friends can still be used even though the child may be unaware of the diagnosis, as the approach focuses on difficulties and behaviour.

- Talk to the focus child about using the approach and obtain the child's consent.

- Parents/carers of the volunteer circle members are also to be informed about their child's involvement in Circle of Friends.

- Whole class meets without the focus child, chaired by an experienced professional (e.g. educational psychologist or SENCO).

- Class to discuss child's strengths and difficulties, creating empathy and sharing own experiences of friendships.

- Recruit volunteers from the class who will form Circle of Friends (6–8 children) who will meet on a weekly basis for 20–30 minutes.

- First meeting of Circle of Friends is with focus child, where rules of group and confidentiality are explained and understood, while setting realistic aims for the group.

- Encourage mutual support, trust, honesty, respect and openness amongst group members.

- Hold weekly meetings to discuss good and bad news related to the focus child, looking at barriers to reaching the aims set by the group and possible solutions.

CAUTION

The Circle of Friends requires facilitation from experienced professionals (Autism Outreach Team Specialist Inclusion services, educational psychologists, SENCOs) in regards to issues such as:

- **Confidentiality:** It is very important to for the Circle of Friends to have mutual support, trust and respect for the focus child (as well as for each other). It is important that the focus child does not become more vulnerable to bullying and exclusion as a result of being part of the Circle of Friends. Sensitive facilitation by the professional is important.

- **Regularity:** Sessions should be regular with a similar format.

- **Safety and benefits for the child with ASD/ensure it's helpful:** Unless skilfully facilitated there are risks that the child may end up feeling even more rejected or be teased should any information be disclosed. Research has shown Circle of Friends increases the confidence of children with ASD in initiating contact with peers, as well as reducing anxiety.

FURTHER READING

Barrett, W., & Randall, L. (2004). Investigating the circle of friends approach: Adaptations and implications for practice. *Educational Psychology in Practice*, 20(4), 353–368.

Carter, C., Meckes, L., Pritchard, L., Swensen, S., Wittman, P. P., & Velde, B. (2004). The friendship club: An after-school program for children with Asperger Syndrome. *Family and Community Health*, 27, 143–150.

Frederickson, N., Warren, L., & Turner, J. (2005). 'Circle of Friends' – An exploration of impact over time. *Educational Psychology in Practice*, 21(3), 197–217.

Gus, L. (2000). Autism: Promoting peer understanding. *Educational Psychology in Practice*, 16(3), 461–468.

Kalyva, E., & Avramidis, E. (2005). Improving communication between children with autism and their peers through the 'Circle of Friends': A small-scale intervention study. *Journal of Applied Research in Intellectual Disabilities*, 18, 253–261.

APPENDIX 10

Personalised Timetable

(Referred to in Chapter 9, Challenging Behaviour and Chapter 6, Planning and Organisation Problems)

What is it for?	To help with organisation and prepare the pupil for change
Who is it for?	Timetable should be created with an adult (secondary school teacher, SENCO, parents/carers)
How is it to be used?	Show how the subjects are matched for either images or colour-coding depending on what the child prefers and can work with
When is it to be used?	To be designed in the first week of secondary school. Child can practise with a blank timetable in primary school and at home with parents/carers.

Below is an alternative personalised timetable adapted from correspondence with Alice Stobart. This can be colour coded for each subject on the timetable. Relevant books or materials also can have a matching coloured sticker so the child knows which things to bring with them to class. If, for example, red is used for maths, the child would have a red maths folder/book and a red sticker on their calculator.

PERSONALIZED TIMETABLE EXAMPLE

	Monday	Tuesday	Wednesday	Thursday	Friday
	REGISTRATION				
9:00–10:00	Maths	PE	English	Maths	PHSE/RE
10:00–11:00	French	English	Biology	Chemistry	Woodwork
11:15–11:30	BREAK				
11:30–12:30	ICT	ICT	Maths	English	Physics
12:30–13:30	LUNCH				
13:30–14:30	Drama	History	French	PE	Art
14:30–15:30	Music	Geography	Maths	History	Cookery

Please also see the Transition Workbook (Appendix 24) which also has advice regarding timetables and how the child can practise using one.

APPENDIX 11

Prompt Cards

(Referred to in Chapter 9, Challenging Behaviour)

What is it for?	To help the child communicate, therefore reducing the likelihood of challenging behaviour
Who is it for?	For the pupil and all the adults involved in supporting the pupil – SENCO, teachers, parents/carers. There should be clear rules agreed between the adults and the pupil as to how to use the prompt card. The consistency in maintaining these rules is pivotal in ensuring the effectiveness of this strategy.
How is it to be used?	The card is used as a visual communication method to inform the teacher that the child feels overwhelmed and would benefit from leaving the classroom for five minutes. Alternative uses for prompt cards could be agreed upon depending on the child's specific needs (for example, if the child is feeling ill or is unable to arrive on time). It is important that clear rules are agreed and established between the teacher and child, such as: ■ The child may feel either comfortable raising the card, leaving the card on the teacher's desk or on the corner of his/her own desk to get the teacher's attention. ■ The child always needs to get an acknowledgement from the teacher that it is OK to leave for five minutes. The teacher may also want to ask the child if they can wait until after class, or perhaps offer an alternative calming technique (e.g. squeezing a stress ball). ■ There needs to be agreement on where the child will be for the five 'time-out' minutes (e.g. standing outside the classroom or in their designated 'safe haven' in the school).
When is it to be used?	This is a proactive strategy which may be helpful in dissipating the lead-up to challenging behaviour and prevent escalation

APPENDIX 12

Lunch Time Activity Timetable

(Referred to in Chapter 9, Challenging Behaviour and Chapter 6, Planning and Organisation)

What is it for?	To help social communication and prevent isolation of a child with ASD
Who is it for?	Introduced and explored by the secondary school teacher, SENCO or TA
How is it to be used?	Look at what options are available for unstructured lunch times and explore the preferences of the child. The child may not need lunch time to be structured for them every day but this should be discussed with the child.
When is it to be used?	At the start of term and reviewed at start of next term

		Monday	Tuesday	Wednesday	Thursday	Friday
Option 1	**Time**	12:00				
	Activity – computing					
	Where	IT Room number X				
	Contact person	Mrs Lamb				

		Monday	Tuesday	Wednesday	Thursday	Friday
Option 2	**Time**	12:30				
	Activity – chess/ games					
	Where	Room 12				
	Contact person	Mr King				

Activity options: football, board games, IT, library, drama club or alternatively offer a quiet room for child to read or draw in.

APPENDIX 13

Buddy System

(Referred to in Chapter 2, Social Interaction)

What is it for?	To help or reduce social isolation in children with ASD
Who is it for?	To set this up, teachers and SENCO should discuss with the child who might be an appropriate buddy and the potential dynamics of peer relationships
How is it to be used?	There may be a variety of ways of doing this, such as having a buddy in the school who is older and is in a different year and/or a buddy who is in the same year. Assign the peer buddy. Give peer buddies information about ASD and ideas to use with students. Modelling strategies can be helpful. Use several peer buddies within a class to reduce the demands on individual children. For older classes, peer buddies could be students enrolled in an elective peer tutoring or peer assistant class.
When is it to be used?	In the first few weeks of secondary school

A buddy system might be helpful for a child who is socially isolated. The aim of this intervention is to identify a socially competent child in the class who ideally has a natural rapport with the child with ASD and can aid the child within the classroom, playground, and in other social situations. It is particularly helpful if the buddy is sociable and popular. Sometimes sensitive advice from peers about what to wear and talk about is more accepted than that from adults. The buddy can, for example, help with the following areas:

- Teach classroom routines (e.g. where to put homework, what to do when arriving in a classroom, where to put materials, etc.)

- Get a classmate involved in a conversation with other children during free time

- Help the child with reading the timetable and to find next classroom (e.g. guiding him/her through hallway).

The buddy system also has benefits for teachers and the child chosen as a buddy. The teachers receive extra support in the classroom. Also, several studies have shown that the child who is helping experiences enhanced personal growth and gains a greater awareness of disability issues.

APPENDIX 14

Emotional Thermometer

*(Referred to in Chapter 8, Anxiety and
Chapter 9, Challenging Behaviour)*

What is it for?	To help the child with ASD communicate how they are feeling
Who is it for?	Should be introduced and practised with an adult (teacher, SENCO, parents/carers). The emotional thermometer may either be used directly by the child to express their feelings or by the teacher to enquire about the child's feelings, by pointing to a place on the scale.
How is it to be used?	This can be used in communicating with the child about their emotional state and helps them to communicate their own emotions
When is it to be used?	To be introduced and practised during a designated quiet time or used in a social skills group. The thermometer can also be used in whole-class situations if agreed by the child and teacher.

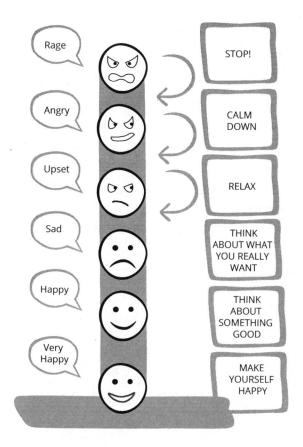

APPENDIX 15

Emotional Toolbox

(Referred to in Chapter 8, Anxiety and Chapter 9, Challenging Behaviour)

What is it for?	To help the child with ASD to recognise and talk about their emotions.
Who is it for?	Should be introduced and practised with an experienced professional (SEN teacher, SENCO)
How is it to be used?	This can be used in helping the child with emotional literacy and to recognise and discuss their own emotions
When is it to be used?	In a social skills group or a setting where an experienced professional can support the child in discussing their emotions

Explore with the child what makes them feel better:

What sorts of things do you like doing when you are happy?

. . . .

. . . .

When do you feel relaxed and what helps you to feel relaxed?

. . . .

. . . .

Describe the emotional toolbox as a set of strategies for dealing with emotions. Explain that it can be used to help a person to recover from a negative emotion. Attwood's toolbox consists of physical activity tools, relaxation tools, social tools, special interests and sensory tools that can help us to 'repair' our feelings when we are anxious/nervous.

EMOTIONAL TOOLBOX

Type of tool	Example			
Activity tools	■ Sport: 'letting off steam' by running, bouncing, stretching ■ Reading a book ■ Working on the computer			
Relaxation tools (see Appendix 22)	■ Deep breathing exercises ■ Spending some time in solitude in a quiet and secluded area ■ Engaging in a repetitive action (e.g. manipulating a stress ball) ■ Tidying a bookshelf (ordering books in alphabetical order)			
Social tools	■ Seeking contact with confidential or designated person ■ Helping others (e.g. explaining something on the computer)			

Source: Adapted from Attwood, (2004).

APPENDIX 16

STAR Record Form

(Referred to in Chapter 9, Challenging Behaviour)

STAR (Setting, Trigger, Action, Result) charts are useful in identifying challenging behaviour and its triggers. It is essential to understand why a child is acting in a certain way and to identify the circumstances where the child is most likely going to act that way.

STAR RECORDING SHEET

Name:_____ Date: _____

Time/Date Monday 1st at 12:00	Setting On the computer	Trigger Another child wants to use the computer	Action Shouting	Results Asked to sit outside the classroom

APPENDIX 17

Sensory Equipment

(Referred to in Chapter 7, Sensory Sensitivities)

What is it for?	To help children with sensory sensitivities
Who is it for?	Should be introduced and practised with an experienced professional (e.g. SEN teacher, SENCO). Parents/carers may also be able to recommend equipment which is known to be useful to the child. Occupational therapists (OTs) are the expert professionals in this area and liaison with an OT, where possible, is also strongly recommended.
How is it to be used?	Equipment can be used in helping the child to cope with sensory sensitivities
When is it to be used?	When deemed appropriate, to reduce stress in a classroom setting or during private relaxation time

COMPANIES THAT SELL SENSORY TOYS AND EQUIPMENT

There are many companies that sell products which can be used to calm or soothe the child with ASD. It is suggested that this equipment is stored in a box in an area which is accessible for the child. The following are some examples:

For tactile sensory sensitivities

ROMPA

Product: Fiddle kit

Contains: A collection of 'fiddle objects' for those who enjoy keeping their hands occupied. Ideal for children with sensory integration problems. A portable, visual, tactile and audible collection.

Cost: £58.69

www.rompa.com/fiddle-kit.html

For tactile and visual sensory sensitivities

TFH Special Needs Toys
Product: Boing Pro – a ball that changes colour when it is squeezed
Cost: £ 7.95
www.specialneedstoys.com/uk/visual/eye-candy/boing-pro-visual-sensory-toy.html

For auditory sensory sensitivities

Ear plugs for children
www.earplugshop.comchildrens-earplugs.html

APPENDIX 18

Bullying Resources

(Referred to in Chapter 5, Bullying)

What is it for?	For children who are or have been bullied or those who are at risk of being bullied
Who is it for?	Bullying strategies should be discussed with the relevant adults (secondary school teacher, SENCO, parents/carers) as well as the child involved
How is it to be used?	Discuss how the strategies will work and get agreement from parents/carers and child
When is it to be used?	The strategies can be used in a proactive or reactive way

HELPFUL RESOURCES

***Bullying and autism spectrum disorders: A guide for school staff* by Alice Stobart:** A booklet which can be purchased from the National Autistic Society website: www.autism.org.uk/products/core-nas-publications/bullying-and-asd.aspx

- **Kidscape:** A registered charity that provides support for children and young people with persistent problems with bullying. It also provides workshops for children and support for school professionals, as well as many helpful resources (www.kidscape.org.uk).

- **Bullying UK:** One of the leading anti-bullying charities in the UK, which works with children, young people, their parents/carers and schools to address bullying, as well as providing very helpful resources for schools (www.bullying.co.uk).

TROUBLE-SHOOTING STRATEGIES

What to do if a child with ASD misinterprets unintentional events as incidents of bullying

Many children with ASD develop heightened anxiety about bullying through their previous experiences. As a difficulty with interpreting social situations is one of the key features of ASD, this problem is not uncommon. However, it is an important issue to address since it causes a high degree of distress to the child and often leads to additional difficulties, such as school refusal, confusion between the school staff and parents/carers, or secondary social difficulties.

- **Ensure that it is a genuine misinterpretation:** Bullies are often socially skilled in disguising their behaviour from teachers, whilst children with ASD are often poor communicators. Reported bullying may therefore be genuine, although difficult to establish. Some forms of bullying can also be very subtle. For example, some children with ASD may have obsessive traits, such as keeping all of their pencils lined up, and persistent disruption of this pattern by others may lead to a significant increase in anxiety. Unobtrusively seeking the views of other children, for example peers from the 'Circle of Friends', can often provide helpful explanations, as children may witness the incidents conducted 'behind the teacher's back'.

- **Psycho-education:** A child with ASD may need help with a clear explanation of what is and what is not bullying. For example, they may need help with understanding what was an accident (e.g. if someone ran into them accidentally) and what was purposeful.

- Children with ASD tend to have difficulty generalising and transferring their learned skills across different situations. Pupils with ASD may therefore need a period of time to learn to distinguish between the two and will need support to reflect on multiple examples or instances of the perceived bullying behaviour. Social Stories, comic strips, pictures, role plays or case vignettes can be very helpful tools (see Appendix 8 for Social Stories).

- **Support:** Children with ASD often have problems with anxiety. Occasionally, although not very often, children with ASD learn strategies which help them to obtain the adult support they need for managing their anxiety or social isolation. For these children, scheduling one-to-one time on a regular basis, even if for a brief period of time, can be a very helpful approach.

- **Treating all incidents separately:** Even when it is established that the child may have a difficulty with misinterpreting social situations, it is important to ensure that all reported incidents are treated separately, as some of them may be genuine.

What to do if a child with ASD is perceived as bully themselves

Difficulties with social insight are one of the key diagnostic features of ASD. As such, children with ASD do not tend to have the ability to manipulate others, spot their weaknesses, or know how to bully others. However, some children with ASD can develop behaviours which can be perceived as bullying. For example, children with ASD can sometimes present with behavioural difficulties, when frustrated. If such difficulties occur, please refer to Chapter 9, Challenging Behaviour.

Goal, Plan, Do, Review

(Referred to in Chapter 6, Planning and Organisation Problems)

What is it for?	To help the pupil with ASD with planning and organisation
Who is it for?	Goal, Plan, Do, Review should be explained by an adult (secondary school teacher, SENCO)
How is it to be used?	In classroom settings
When is it to be used?	When needed

Goal **What do I need to do?**	Plan **How will I do it?**	Do **When will I do it?**	Review? **How did it go?**

PROMPT CARD

At the start of the lesson I should:	**At the end of the lesson I should:**
1. Wait outside the classroom with the others until the teacher asks us to come in 2. Sit at my desk 3. Get the books we need 4. Get out my pencil case 5. Listen to the teacher carefully. I can ask the teacher or a teaching assistant if I do not understand what I have to do. I do this by putting up my hand.	1. Check if there is any homework. If there is, I should write it in my diary 2. Put all my books and my pencil case in my bag 3. Look at my timetable to see what I am doing next and where I need to go. I should ask the teacher or a teaching assistant if I do not know what to do, or where I need to go next.

APPENDIX 20

Homework

(Referred to in Chapter 6, Planning and Organisation Problems)

What is it for?	To help organise and prioritise homework assignments
Who is it for?	Homework strategies should be explained by an adult in the school (secondary school teacher, SENCO) in collaboration with the parents/carers
How is it to be used?	Show how the homework is going to be organised and what is required to help the child work through it. Identify how long to spend on parts of homework and what the priorities are
When is it to be used?	To be explained in the first week of secondary school with weekly revisions depending on homework amount and type

Most children with ASD benefit from clear rules and tend to adhere to these conscientiously. It can therefore be surprising to learn how many misunderstandings can be caused by pupils' difficulties with completing homework. In most cases this is not due to a child's lack of concern or interest, but due to underlying difficulties with aspects such as self-organisation or language skills. An awareness that this can be an issue even for very academically able pupils with ASD, coupled with the application of simple support strategies, can be very effective in preventing frustration for teachers and pupils alike.

- **Self-organisation:** Ensure that the pupil has noted down the assignment title, due date and the materials they may need to complete it. Some pupils may need to mark it directly in their schedule, to ensure they will be able to balance demands placed on them in different subjects.

- **Time allocation:** Children with ASD can often find it difficult to switch from one topic to another, without fixating on details and losing the general picture. They may also display perfectionism. This may result in pupils spending an excessive amount of time on one assignment and consequently running out of time to complete others. If this is the case, the pupil may benefit from help with time allocation for each assignment, so that they can appropriately distribute their effort and time across all subject areas.

- **Prioritisation:** ASD is often associated with strong interests. Whilst this often leads to a child with ASD developing impressive knowledge and skills in certain areas, it can also result in them having reduced motivation to work on other important areas of the curriculum. Varying interest and motivation is not unusual in typically developing children. However, some pupils with ASD can have strong fixations and significant problems with shifting their attention to other areas. Prioritising work, starting with subjects children are the least interested in, and using the area of special interest as a motivator once other work is completed, can be a useful strategy.

- **Involving parents/carers:** Parents are often very keen to help with ensuring their children's homework is completed on time. If parents are informed about the homework assignments they can often help their child to overcome their difficulties with organisation.

APPENDIX 21

Explaining the Diagnosis of ASD to the Child: A Handout for Parents/Carers

*(Referred to in Chapter 1, General Support
with the Transition to Secondary School)*

Understandably, this is a very sensitive issue for most parents/carers and professionals. At the time when the child is first assessed, the concept of ASD can seem very abstract for most young children. Also, their parents/carers may need time to process the assessment findings, to learn about the impact of the condition, and work on ensuring that their child's support needs are being met. In fact, research indicates that this last issue in particular is the most common reason for parents/carers requesting an assessment and a formal diagnosis. However, as the focus is being placed on supporting the child with their areas of difficulty, parents/carers often receive very little guidance or help as to how to introduce the topic of diagnosis to their child. This handout is therefore aimed at highlighting the main factors to be weighed up in considering whether or not to share the diagnosis, how to go about sharing the diagnosis, as well as advice regarding the timing of the discussion for the parents/carers and teachers. As there is currently a very limited amount of research literature available on this issue, and as each child and family will need to view things from their individual perspective, this handout will focus on outlining the main issues and ways to think about and deal with these in general.

WHEN IS THE RIGHT TIME TO TALK TO THE CHILD ABOUT THE DIAGNOSIS?

Unfortunately, there are no clear guidelines based on empirical research which would enable us to provide a direct estimate of the best time to discuss the diagnosis with the child. This will depend on a number of factors, all of which can impact on the suitable timing of the discussion. These include the child's maturity, cognitive level and curiosity, as well as the readiness of parents/carers to share the diagnosis. The level of support available from the wider social network is another important factor. However, as children grow older, their horizons start shifting from their immediate needs and wishes, to beginning to perceive the perspectives of others as well. Although this process might be somewhat delayed for children with ASD, children on the autistic spectrum also find peer comparison and reference to others important for the formation of their own identity, as is evident from research findings.

As children get older, they start to compare themselves with their peers. The complexity of their comparisons can vary depending on their maturity, social awareness, and their cognitive and developmental level. Children with ASD, especially higher functioning children in mainstream schools, gradually start perceiving certain differences between themselves and their peers. These comparisons can sometimes be positive, and sometimes less favorable. For example, sometimes they may begin to wonder why they are finding some things much easier or harder than their peers. Sometimes they may be worried by not being able to fit in with their peers as easily as other children. Other times they may ask how other children seem to understand the rules of a game, which were never clearly explained. Or they may question why they have a supporting adult next to them during the lessons or at break times. Occasionally they may simply repeat the perceptions of other children about them, such as why they have to do certain things in certain ways.

When children start wondering about these issues, they often begin to seek explanations, even if they may not verbalise their thoughts. If children do not understand the reasons for certain differences, there is a risk that their own explanations may not be helpful (for example, that they are less clever than their peers) and may not result in them generating helpful management strategies (e.g. 'I always get picked on and there is nothing I can do about it'). However, the more children really understand the issue, the more they can be supported in developing coping strategies. Whilst it is not possible to pinpoint the ideal time when one should disclose the diagnosis to the child, the following points can prove to be important and helpful indicators:

- The child with ASD is beginning to ask about other children or comparing themselves with their peers.

- Peers are beginning to ask questions about the child's unique ways of perceiving things around them, or their particular behaviours.

- Special arrangements need to be put in place to support the child (e.g. one-to-one support in the classroom) which may cause the question of additional educational needs to arise.

- The child is at risk of developing low self-esteem. The child would benefit from having an understanding of their unique strengths and being equipped with coping strategies which could help them to overcome their difficulties.

- The child may benefit from attending a specific programme for children with ASD (e.g. social skills group) or from having opportunities to meet like-minded peers.

- Parents/carers have had an opportunity to process the diagnosis and internalise not only the risk factors, but also the strengths and positive aspects of ASD.

- The child is becoming more independent and can gradually be introduced to self-management strategies to help them to cope effectively.

- If the child's intellectual curiosity is one of their main strengths, providing them with appropriate information and reading materials written by other young people with ASD can often be beneficial. Having access to this informs their identity and strengthens their coping and self-esteem.

By the time children are approaching the transition to secondary school, some or most of these factors may have come into play. Given that there will be an increased emphasis on self-management in the secondary school, sharing the diagnosis well in advance is recommended. This should allow sufficient time for the child to process the information in a familiar environment where they feel secure and where they know the routines.

Although the issue of sharing the diagnosis can understandably raise parent/carer anxiety, it is important to be aware that the child will have to learn this information at some point. In planning this proactively, parents/carers will need to consider the longer-term timeline. It may be wise to avoid introducing the diagnosis for the first time during a stage of development which is complex and demanding itself, such as puberty. As a general guideline, holding this discussion prior to child's transition to secondary school is advisable. However, this may have to be adjusted depending on the child's and family's unique circumstances.

MAIN CONCERNS AND HOW TO DEAL WITH THEM

Based on clinical experience, parents/carers of children with ASD tend to be mainly concerned about the impact of the diagnosis on the child's self-esteem, identity and sense of belonging within their peer group. They worry that sharing the diagnosis may cause the child to feel stigmatised at school. Although this list may not be exhaustive, it aims to address the most frequent issues raised by parents, children and professionals:

- **Impact on self-esteem:** As the child's wellbeing is of paramount importance to most parents/carers, concerns about the impact on their child's self-esteem are certainly justified. However, the more open that parents/carers are able to be in discussing the child's difficulties with them, the more they will be able to help the child to deal with these positively and constructively. Children who are unaware of the reasons for some of their difficulties are at risk of coming to unfavourable and generalised conclusions about themselves. For example, if they have difficulties with PE and with making friends, they are at risk of thinking that they are 'not good' or 'stupid'. However, if the parents/carers are able to talk to them openly, this will provide them with an invaluable opportunity to facilitate a more balanced approach in their thinking. This may include pointing out that whilst these specific difficulties are associated with ASD, children who have this way of thinking about the world also have many unique strengths (such as attention to detail, loyalty, responsibility, specific interests, etc.). As such, talking about the diagnosis in a balanced way can help to deal with the child's immediate concerns and is helpful in preventing low self-esteem.

- **Identity:** Many people raise concerns that knowledge of the diagnosis can negatively impact on the child's identity. For instance, they may worry that the child will start perceiving themselves as having a serious disability and therefore stop trying their best. Whilst this is a valid concern, there are many helpful ways to prevent this from happening. Recent campaigns aimed at facilitating inclusion can provide plenty of useful, creative and attractive resources for young people. Lots of celebrities, media stars and exceptionally successful people considered as very 'cool' and acceptable by younger generations have disclosed their difficulties and diagnoses such as ADHD (Will Smith, Steven Spielberg and Mohammad Ali), dyslexia (Orlando Bloom, Keira Knightley, and Tom Cruise), and ASD (Satoshi Tajiri, creator of Pokémon; Jim Henson, creator of the Muppets). Not only can they act as very appealing role models, but their life stories can also provide inspiration in dealing with adversity and managing to succeed in life despite significant challenges. Most children with ASD enjoy using their computers and searching for these positive examples on the internet.

This can be an enjoyable and empowering journey both for the children as well as their parents/carers.

- **Sense of difference:** It is true that awareness of the diagnosis can sometimes foster a sense of difference in a child. However, by the end of their primary school years most children with ASD already have a perception that they are in some way different to their peers. This can often be concerning or isolating for them. So long as it is introduced appropriately, having a knowledge and an understanding of the diagnosis can be a source of reassurance for the child. It can be comforting for the child to know that there are many other children with similar difficulties and strengths. It can provide the child with a useful reference group and opportunities to meet like-minded peers. Frequently, children will enjoy exchanging information with peers with ASD over the internet by means of NAS forums or through support groups available at school or in the neighbourhood. Through being able to talk about this openly, parents/carers can also help the child to develop a sense of difference in a positive way. Public opinion and awareness of ASD has increased and improved significantly over the past decades and there are also many programmes aimed at highlighting the special strengths of children/adults with ASD, such as Tony Attwood's 'ASPIE' programme (Attwood, 2004).

HOW TO EXPLAIN THE DIAGNOSIS TO THE CHILD

Each parent/carer knows their own child best, which makes them the expert in maximising the child's strengths and scaffolding for their difficulties as needed. ASD is a complex diagnosis which can present itself in so many unique ways for each person and there is currently no single 'best way' to explain the diagnosis to the child. However, parents/carers should be encouraged to rely on their knowledge of their child and to use the communication methods to which the child is most responsive. The following are general principles which may be helpful to consider in preparing for this discussion:

- **Parent/carer perception of diagnosis:** Children tend to make sense of the world around them based on their own previous experience of it, coupled with the messages they receive from others. Parents/carers should therefore allow themselves sufficient time to process the diagnosis first before considering discussion of the diagnosis with the child. Parents/carers should allow themselves time to come to terms with issues of concern to them. If the parents/carers are extremely worried or tearful when talking about the diagnosis, the child may become overwhelmed and gain a sense that it is something they themselves should be worried about too. The journey taken in coming to terms with the diagnosis will vary greatly from parent to parent and will usually depend on a number of factors, particularly the circumstances in which the family finds itself at the time of the diagnosis and also the history of the child's difficulties prior to diagnosis. Parents/carers should feel free to seek additional support or advice from the clinician or team making the diagnosis and from associations such as the National Autistic Society. Once parents/carers have had an opportunity to genuinely familiarise themselves with the positive aspects of this condition and have gained knowledge of a range of positive coping strategies, they will be able to convey their optimism and balanced perception of ASD to their child.

- **Communication issues:** Some children will have no difficulty discussing the topic of diagnosis with their parents/carers, whilst others may benefit from having visual resources to facilitate their comprehension. Parents/carers of children who communicate best with the additional use of visual materials could therefore consider developing a diary or a 'little book about me' with the child.

- **Introducing the concept that everyone has some strengths and difficulties:** Concrete examples of the child's favourite celebrities or relatives and friends around them can add meaning and validity to this statement.

- **Introducing the concept that special needs and ASD are not rare and that children with special needs or ASD can do equally well in life:** Again, using concrete examples and role models may be inspiring for children.

- **Balance between strengths and difficulties:** When introducing a concept that the child may find difficult, it is always helpful to think about their particular strengths and possible coping strategies (for example, if child finds it difficult to express their emotions, it can be helpful to emphasise that they have an exceptional vocabulary when talking about their specialist interest, and remind them that they can use a card system or pictures to let others know how they feel).

- **Concrete visual examples:** When talking about the child's strengths, difficulties and coping strategies in a particular area, it might be useful to set up a table with three columns to help the child link these together.

- **Other children with ASD:** If the child knows someone with a diagnosis of ASD who has different needs to them, they may find it harder to identify with the diagnosis or with how it applies to them. For example, if another pupil at the school has autism as well as learning disability or challenging behaviour, these distinctions may need to be explained to the child to help them to understand that each child is unique, even if they may have something in common. Whilst friendships with other peers with ASD with similar interests can be encouraged, it cannot be assumed that children will get on even if they have similar support needs (see Chapter 2, Social Interaction).

- **Explaining what ASD is not, as well as what ASD is:** When explaining the diagnosis, parents/carers should also consider 'spelling out' what is not part of ASD. Many children with ASD can have additional difficulties which are not part of ASD, even if it may be associated with it in some ways. For example, it may be important for children to know that anxiety does not have to be part of ASD and that they can get help with it.

APPENDIX 22

Relaxation Strategies

(Referred to in Chapter 8, Anxiety)

What is it for?	To help reduce anxiety in children
Who is it for?	These strategies can be introduced by an adult (secondary school teacher, SENCO, parents/carers)
How is it to be used?	In discussion with the child with ASD find strategies which are useful to them
When is it to be used?	When necessary, when emotions become overwhelming and before behaviour has become challenging or anxiety too great

The next pages consist of very useful techniques and strategies for helping children to think about their emotions and describe how to reduce anxiety and enhance relaxation.

Be the boss of your feelings!

From the morning until the evening, everything that happens during the day can make us have lots of different feelings. For example:

John wakes up and feels excited as it is the weekend and he is going to visit his grandparents.

It is very normal to want to feel good all the time. When we think we are going to feel bad, we might try and do things to make us feel better straight away.

John is worried about being late, so he asks his mum when they are leaving which helps him feel relieved.

But sometimes, we cannot tell when something is going to happen or how it is going to make us feel because it is unexpected.

The car won't start, which makes John angry. His parents decide that they will have to get the train instead. John becomes worried as he does not like noisy, crowded places.

	(☑ or ☒)
Do you ever feel like the bad feelings are getting too strong, or 'taking over'?	
Do you ever feel like you are missing out on good feelings?	

If you ticked either of these, you may want to be *the boss of your feelings*! We can still do the things we want to do even when unexpected things happen.

John tells his mum he would rather stay at home, but she suggests that he brings his headphones to distract him from the busy train. This makes him feel relaxed, and he feels proud that he was able to be the boss of his feelings.

How do I relax?

Knowing how to relax is one of the best ways to become the boss of your feelings. There are lots of methods to try that work differently and for different situations. Finding out which one suits you can help you to *be the boss.*

Relax with your body	**Relax with your mind**
Being active ■ Do some exercise, e.g. sets of star jumps or press-ups ■ Play a sport, e.g. football, tennis These are natural ways of tensing and relaxing your muscles	*Chilling out* ■ Read a book ■ Watch a clip that inspires you ■ Use relaxation apps on your tablet ■ Listen to chill-out music
Deep breaths 1. Take in a deep breath 2. Hold it for five seconds 3. Let it out slowly 4. Concentrate on how it feels	*Imagination* This is when you… 1. Shut your eyes 2. Think of your favourite place or thing 3. Imagine you are there and concentrate on the things that make you happy
Muscle stretching 1. Find somewhere quiet 2. Squeeze/tense an area of muscles and hold for a few seconds 3. Let go and notice how it feels when your muscles relax The idea is to go from a stiff scarecrow to a relaxed ragdoll	

Stretching the body

Pick a part of your body first. Clench the muscles for five seconds, then stretch, let go and release.

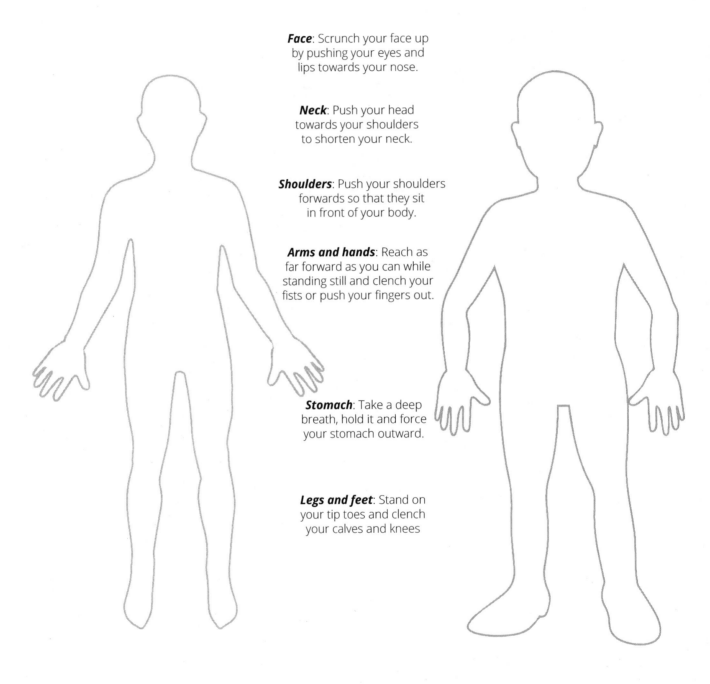

Face: Scrunch your face up by pushing your eyes and lips towards your nose.

Neck: Push your head towards your shoulders to shorten your neck.

Shoulders: Push your shoulders forwards so that they sit in front of your body.

Arms and hands: Reach as far forward as you can while standing still and clench your fists or push your fingers out.

Stomach: Take a deep breath, hold it and force your stomach outward.

Legs and feet: Stand on your tip toes and clench your calves and knees

The feelings detective

Even when we have strategies to *be the bosses of our feelings*, there are some times when we cannot use them quickly enough and the feelings take over. If we can spot the clues that tell us a feeling is going to take over, we can be *feelings detectives* to help us to *be the boss* again. Try to follow these steps to be a *feelings detective*:

1. Think about the last time you had a bad feeling. What was it? Tick below.

    ☐ Sadness ☐ Anger ☐ Anxiety Other: . . . .

2. Did the bad feeling make your body feel different? Where in your body?

    ☐ Head ☐ Tummy ☐ Legs Other: . . . .

3. Investigate this bad feeling by asking others if they have felt it. How do they make themselves feel better?

    . . . .

    . . . .

    . . . .

    Make a list of clues from your investigation. Do similar things happen each time?

Feelings ladders

By finding the clues in our body and our thoughts, and writing them all down, we can *detect*, or notice, what might happen when feelings are taking over. As the feeling gets stronger, it may feel like you are climbing a ladder, becoming less safe as you get further away from the ground.

JOHN'S FEELINGS LADDERS

John decided to draw feelings ladders to remind himself how he dealt with the car breaking down and having to get the train to his grandparents' house.

He was able to stop himself getting to the top of the ladder, and climb back down to the bottom, by spotting the clues, such as getting sweaty and feeling angry, and using strategies.

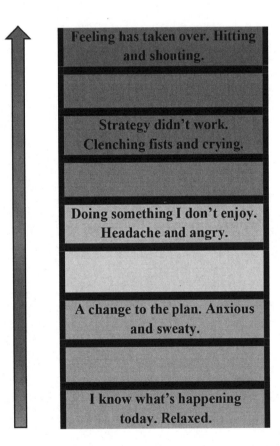

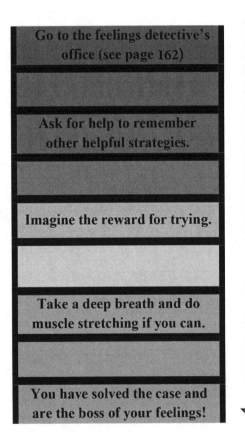

The next time John thinks a feeling is taking over, he can be a *feelings detective* by looking for the same clues, and use strategies to relax.

Try your own feelings ladder on the next page!

Make your own feelings ladders!

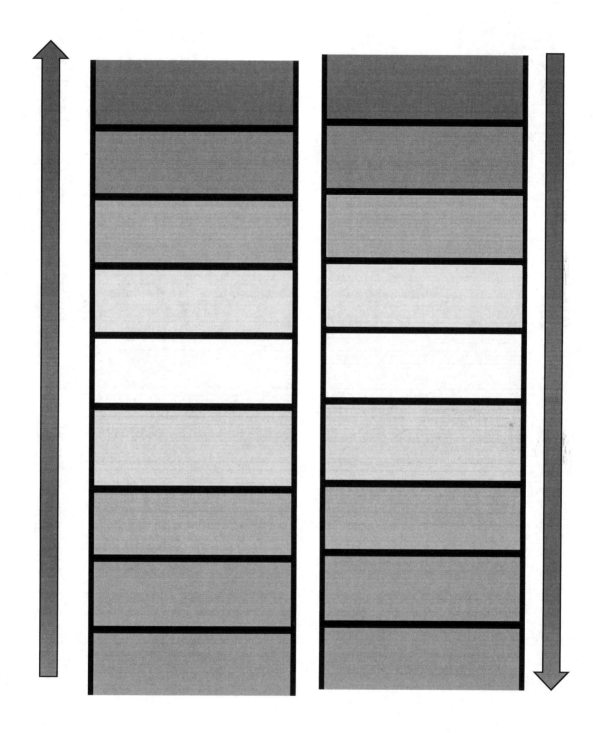

The feelings detective's office

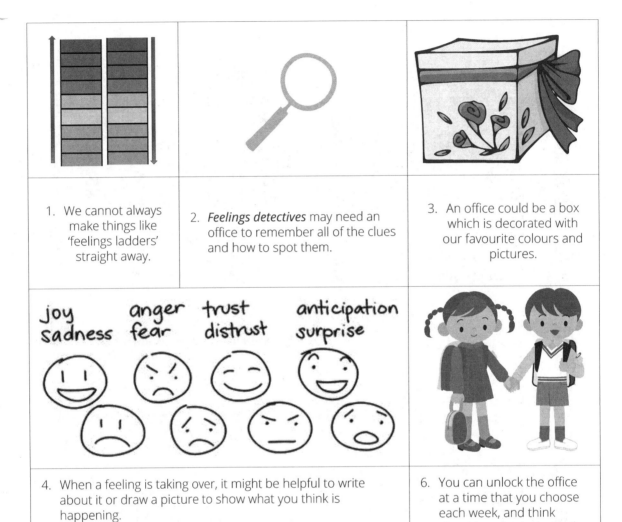

1. We cannot always make things like 'feelings ladders' straight away.

2. *Feelings detectives* may need an office to remember all of the clues and how to spot them.

3. An office could be a box which is decorated with our favourite colours and pictures.

4. When a feeling is taking over, it might be helpful to write about it or draw a picture to show what you think is happening.

5. It can be locked away in the feelings detective's office until you are ready to think about it and to make you feel safer.

6. You can unlock the office at a time that you choose each week, and think about how to deal with the feeling, or talk to someone you trust about it.

Relaxation for younger children

THE COPYCAT GAME

Muscle stretching can be practised by imitating different animals and targeting specific body parts:

- *Face*: a monkey pulling a funny face or an angry lion.

- *Neck*: a giraffe reaching for fruit on the highest branch.

- *Shoulders*: a turtle hiding its head in its shell.

- *Arms and hands*: a tree stretching its branches as wide or a bird spreading its wings.

- *Stomach*: a frog sticking its belly out as it breathes in.

- *Legs and feet*: a cheetah getting ready to accelerate and pounce.

By the end of the game, the children should flop like jellyfishes on the floor to fully relax the body.

Picture yourself

Imagination can be used to help the child to relax by shutting their eyes and pretending that they are drawing a scene with all of their favourite things. Guide them along the way by giving instructions such as 'pick up your pencil' and 'draw the things you would need to do your favourite activity'. Ask them about how a certain sense is feeling, for example what they can smell, then draw attention to how relaxed their body is feeling. They can revisit their scene at any time and it will become more relaxing with practice.

Don't worry if imagining is not easy – have a go at drawing a place that you would enjoy below and use it to play the game!

APPS AND VIDEOS

- **Smiling Mind:** This app is full of meditation exercises designed for children as young as seven years old. It also asks how you are feeling pre- and post-meditation and shows your progress, which tells you how close you are to being the boss of your feelings.

- **TheHonestGuys (YouTube):** this is a popular YouTube channel with hundreds of guided meditation, relaxation and sleep videos as well as calming music from scenes that may inspire ideas for 'Picture yourself'.

APPENDIX 23

Skills and Abilities

(Used Chapter 6, Planning and Organisation)

Thinking about this child, does (s)he have serious difficulties in these areas? Are these difficulties much worse than those of most classmates?

Skill	Description	Signs that skill is impaired	Present
Goal setting	Identifying or setting appropriate goal	Problems understanding how to approach open-ended complex tasks (e.g. coursework) 'Future blindness'	
Planning	Coming up with a plan to work towards a goal	Rushes into tasks without thinking Starts projects without a plan/necessary materials Begins task and then does not know what to do next	
Sequencing	Doing things step-by-step, in the right order	Skips steps in multi-part activity Does things in the wrong order Has trouble telling a story	
Prioritising	Allocating time to tasks according to their importance	Spends all their time on one small part of an overall task Trouble with note-taking, knowing which bits to record and which to leave out	
Organisation	Managing the materials needed to work towards goals	Arrives at lessons without necessary materials Loses stuff all the time Desk, bag or locker is really messy	
Initiating	Getting started	Cannot independently get going when given a task (e.g. 'just sits there')	
Inhibition	Avoiding short-term distraction in the service of a long-term goal	Easily distracted Loses sight of goals and focuses on the short term More motivated by short-term rewards	
Pace	Managing time	Often runs out of time on a task, or finishes much too quickly	

cont.

Skill	Description	Signs that skill is impaired	Present
Flexibility	Moving from one activity or train of thought to another when working towards a goal	Gets stuck on one activity and so does not progress Struggles at points of transition (e.g. between class and break) Disturbed by unexpected changes in routine	
Self-monitoring	Keeping track of performance, comparing performance to the goal and plan	Does not check for or notice own mistakes Persists with ineffective strategies	
Emotion control	Regulating own emotions to allow continued working towards a goal	Child is easily moved to extreme emotions, and this gets in the way of their work	
Completing	Finishing tasks that have been started	Child rarely finishes tasks without constant reminders and support	
Evaluating	Comparing performance to the goal and plan	Struggles with being objective about own performance Does not review own work without support	

APPENDIX 24

My Transition Workbook

You may want to stick or draw a picture of yourself or your new school here:

My name is: . . . .

My primary school is called: . . . .

My secondary school is called: . . . .

Introduction

What does 'transition' mean?

The word 'transition' means *the process of change*. For example, a transition could be changing from primary school to secondary school. In a time of transition (or change), some things can be exciting, and other things can be quite worrying. However, **planning** for the transition can make changes much less frightening with the help of other people.

What is this workbook for?

With your transition to secondary school approaching, this workbook is here to help you plan the move to your next school. Your parents/carers, and teachers at your primary school, can also help you complete it.

Some parts of the workbook are here to gather some useful information, some parts will help you think about what you are looking forward to, and some parts will help you make a plan to help with any things you might be worried about.

Everyone has different strengths and worries, so some pages might be more important for you, and some not so much. It is OK to leave these pages blank. Just fill in the pages that have things on them that are important to you.

We hope you find the workbook useful and you enjoy completing the activities that we have set for you.

Have fun!

Key:

Whenever you see the pencil 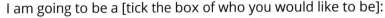 symbol it shows you that you might like to draw, colour or stick in something (like a picture or diagram) on the page.

This transition workbook can be used like a map to investigate your move to secondary school. To do this, why not choose who you want to be before we start the investigation?

I am going to be a [tick the box of who you would like to be]:

☐ Detective

☐ Scientist

☐ Investigator

☐ Someone who likes to know stuff!

☐ ....

Who would you like to be?

Fact finding about my new school

To help you with your transition to secondary school, it might be helpful to search for clues about your new school. Some things you might want to find out are written below:

About my new school:

School name: ....

Address: ....

....

Telephone number: ....

About my new teachers:

My head teacher is called:..

My form teacher is called: ....

Other important people in my new school:

....

....

....

What I am looking forward to the most

In a new school there might be many opportunities to try out things you have never done before, or to learn more about things you are good at.

You may have already been asked to think about three things that you are looking forward to about moving to secondary school. It may be helpful to copy these things on the lines below so that they can be kept as a reminder for you, and other people who you will meet at your new school.

The three main things I am excited about moving to secondary school are:

1. . . . .

. . . .

. . . .

2. . . . .

. . . .

. . . .

3. . . . .

. . . .

. . . .

The treasure chest

There might be lots of other things that you are excited about, or are looking forward to, about moving to secondary school. You might like to use the treasure chest below to write or draw these things here; there are a few examples to help get you going:

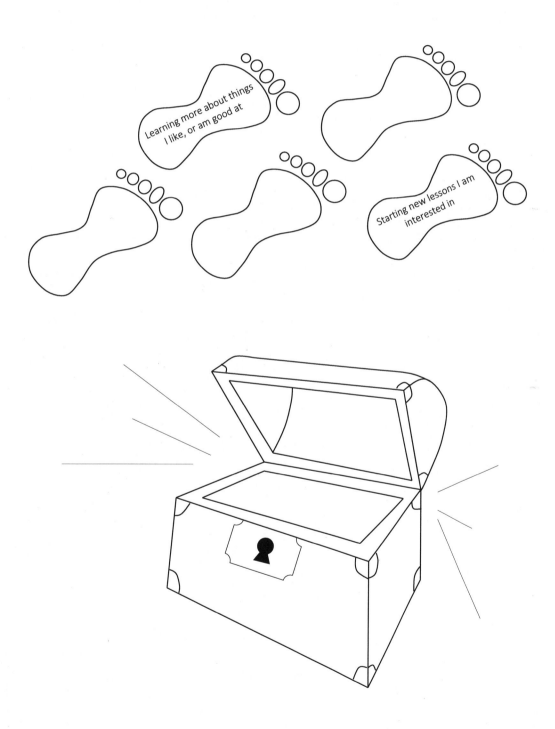

My biggest worries

Starting new things can be exciting but they can also be quite scary. It is good to investigate what these worries are so that you can plan what to do about them.

You may have already been asked to think about three things that you are not looking forward to about moving to secondary school. It may be helpful to copy these things on the lines below so that they can be kept as a reminder for you, and other people who can help you with them.

The three main things I am worried about moving to secondary school are:

1. . . . .

. . . .

. . . .

2. . . . .

. . . .

. . . .

3. . . . .

. . . .

. . . .

The worry-cloud

There might be lots of other things that you could be worried about moving to secondary school. You may have already been given a list of things that some children feel worried about when they move to secondary school. You might like to use the worry-cloud below to write those worries here too so you can share them with people who can help; there are a few examples to help get you going:

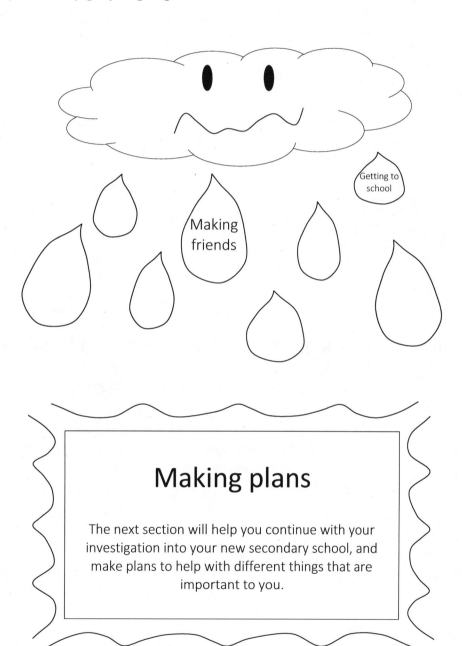

Getting to school

Making friends

Making plans

The next section will help you continue with your investigation into your new secondary school, and make plans to help with different things that are important to you.

Finding some assistants

When you are doing an investigation, are on an expedition, or when you are trying to find out stuff, you will need the help of some assistants (people who can help and support you).

Who can assist me on my transition to secondary school?

I think these people will be good assistants to help me with my transition to secondary school [tick the box(es) of who you think would be the best assistants]:

☐ My mum or dad

☐ My older brother or sister

☐ A cousin or other family member who has just been through the transition to secondary school

☐ My primary school teacher(s)

☐ The SENCO at my primary school

☐ One of my older friends

☐ Someone else:

. . . .

Who is going to be my key assistant from my new secondary school?

You may want to ask for help from your parents or one of your primary school teachers to find out who your key assistant is going to be at your new secondary school.

You may want to stick or draw a picture of your key assistant here:

Name: . . . .

Job title: . . . .

How to find them: . . . .

When to find them: . . . .

Getting to my new secondary school

I am going to travel to my new school by [tick the correct box]:

☐ Walking

☐ Bike

☐ Car

☐ Bus

☐ Tube (underground train)

☐ Train

☐ I am going to travel with: . . . .

Planning my timing:

The *school day starts* at:

and *ends* at:

To get to school on time, I would need to *leave the house* at:

To leave the house on time, I would *need to get up* at:

Getting to know my new secondary school

It may be important to you to find out a bit more about your new secondary school. This might include things like visiting your new school, finding out information before you start at the school, or making plans to help you with things you want to find out more about when you start at the school.

Visiting my new secondary school

I am visiting my new school on: __ __ / __ __ / __ __ __ __ at

Who will come with you when you visit your new school? tick the correct box:

☐ My mum or dad

☐ My older brother or sister

☐ A cousin or other family member who has just been through the transition to secondary school

☐ My primary school teacher(s)

☐ The SENCO at my primary school

☐ One of my older friends

☐ Someone else:

. . . .

Who will you meet when you visit your new school? (You may need to ask the person you chose as your assistant(s) with finding this out.)

. . . .

. . . .

After your visit to your new secondary school:

How did the visit to your new secondary school go?

. . . .

. . . .

Did anything make you excited?

. . . .

. . . .

Did anything make you worried?

. . . .

. . . .

Are there any things you need to remember?

. . . .

. . . .

. . . .

Are there any things you would like help with?

. . . .

. . . .

. . . .

School rules

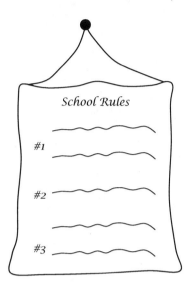

Every school may have different rules. As you get older, there might be new rules to learn about. It is important to remember that school rules are there to make school life better for everyone.

If a school rule is broken there may be consequences (results) that you will need to know about. For some schools, if a rule is broken it may mean that the person who broke the rule is not allowed out at break or lunch time. For other schools, if someone breaks a rule it may mean that that person gets a detention (which could mean that they spend some extra time at school after the normal school day is finished).

There are sometimes ways that you can make things better/fix a situation after a school rule has been broken. Sometimes this might be simple, like saying sorry; other times it may mean that you spend some of your own time fixing something that has been broken.

It might be important to you to check what the rules are at your secondary school so you can start learning them, plan how to follow them, and know what to do if you break them.

☐ I would like to find out about the rules at my new secondary school in advance i.e. before I get there [tick the box if you agree].

☐ I would like to find out about what happens if I break a school rule [tick the tox if you agree].

☐ I would like to find out about what to do/how I could fix the situation if I break a school rule [tick the box if you agree].

If you ticked any of the box(es) above:
Who could help/assist you with finding out more about the rules at your new secondary school?

. . . .

After you have found out more about the rules at your new secondary school:

How did finding out about the new school rules go?

. . . .

. . . .

Did anything make you excited?

. . . .

. . . .

Did anything make you worried?

. . . .

. . . .

Are there any things you need to remember?

. . . .

. . . .

. . . .

Are there any things you would like help with?

. . . .

. . . .

. . . .

Getting to know the staff (teachers) in my new secondary school

In primary school (where you are at school now), you may have one main teacher (usually called your classroom teacher).

You may also have a teaching assistant (TA) who helps out in your classroom, as well as perhaps having other teachers for different lessons like Maths or English.

When children go to secondary school, they will usually have a different teacher for different lessons like Maths, English, Geography, History and lots more. This can be quite exciting but can also be quite scary.

Some people like to meet the teachers they are going to be working with before they start at the new secondary school. This might be important for you too.

☐ I would like to find out about the teachers I will have at my new secondary school in advance i.e. before I get there [tick the box if you agree].

☐ I would like to meet the teachers who will be teaching me [tick the box if you agree].

If you ticked either of the box(es) above:
Who could help/assist you with finding out more about the teachers you will have in your new secondary school?

. . . .

After you have found out more about the teachers you will have in your new secondary school:

How did finding out about your new teachers go?

. . . .

. . . .

Did anything make you excited?

. . . .

. . . .

. . . .

Did anything make you worried?

. . . .

. . . .

. . . .

Are there any things you need to remember?

. . . .

. . . .

. . . .

Are there any things you would like help with?

. . . .

. . . .

. . . .

You may want to write a list of your new teachers here:

My secondary school teachers picture board:

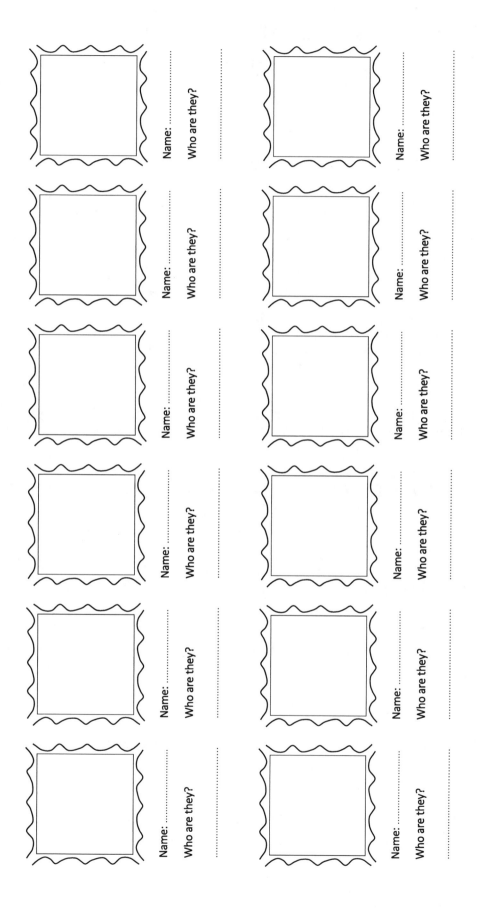

Getting to know my way around my new secondary school

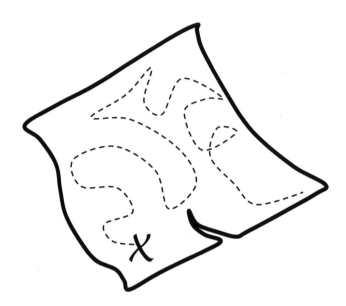

One of the things that lots of children are worried about when they make the transition to secondary school is how big their new school is. Often children are worried about not being able to find their classroom and getting lost.

Like many other children, you might also be worried about how big your new secondary school is. It may be important for you to plan ahead and think about getting or making a map of your new school to help you feel less worried.

☐ I would like to get to know my way around my new secondary school in advance i.e. before I get there [tick the box if you agree].

☐ I would like to get, or create, a map of my new secondary school [tick the box if you agree].

If you ticked either of the box(es) above:
Who could help/assist you with finding out more about how to get around your new secondary school?

. . . .

After you have found out more about getting around your new secondary school:

How did finding out about getting around your new school go?

. . . .

. . . .

. . . .

Did anything make you excited?

. . . .

. . . .

. . . .

Did anything make you worried?

. . . .

. . . .

. . . .

Are there any things you need to remember?

. . . .

. . . .

. . . .

Are there any things you would like help with?

. . . .

. . . .

. . . .

You may want to stick or draw a map of your new school here

Getting to know my new timetable

Time	Monday	Tuesday	Wednesday	Thursday	Friday
08:00					
09:00					
10:00					
11:00					
12:00					
13:00					
14:00					
15:00					

At primary school you will have had a few lessons in a week and you will have learnt which days and what times those lessons happen. For example, English might have been on a Tuesday morning, Maths might have been on a Thursday morning, and PE might have been on a Wednesday afternoon.

At secondary school you will have more lessons to go to, perhaps five or six every day. You will also have a lot more teachers. You will usually have one teacher for each subject/ topic (e.g. Maths, Science, Geography). With many more teachers to get used to, you might find the 'secondary school teachers picture board' on page 183 extra helpful.

It is important to check whether your new secondary school has a one- or two-week timetable. If it has a two-week timetable you will also need to remember which week you need to follow, i.e. the timetable for 'Week 1', or 'Week 2'. It might be *useful to get a calendar* that has all the weeks of a month on one page so you can plan out which weeks you need to follow the 'Week 1' timetable, and which weeks you need to follow the 'Week 2' timetable.

Your new timetable is one of the most important things you will need when you start at your new secondary school.

Your new timetable will show you:

Time	Monday
08:00	
	School starts
09:00	Assembly
10:00	Maths Room 1 LW
11:00	Break
12:00	English Room 2 MM
13:00	Lunch
14:00	PE (double lesson) Sports Hall
15:00	WM

- *Which* lessons you have on which day.

- What *time* the lessons start and end.
  (Getting a watch if you haven't got one might be useful to help you practise telling the time and getting to/from different places so you won't be late to your lessons.)

- Which *room* the lessons are in.
  (Some lessons might be in specific rooms e.g. PE might be in a sports hall, Food technology might be in a special kitchen, and Science might be in a laboratory.)

- Which *teacher* you will have for each subject/topic.
  (This might be written as just the initials of the teacher, e.g. 'Mr J. Bloggs' might be written as 'JB'.)

Because the timetable shows you all of these things, it can help you prepare when packing your school bag with the things you need for the next day.

It might be important to you to get a copy of your new timetable before you start at your new secondary school. Some schools may not have got this ready for you just yet, so it might be useful to get the timetable that the current Year 7 pupils (children in their first year of secondary school) are following.

☐ I would like to get a copy of my new timetable in advance i.e. before I start my new secondary school [tick the box if you agree].

☐ If my new timetable is not ready, I would like to get a copy of the timetable that the current Year 7 pupils have [tick the box if you agree].

If you ticked either of the box(es) above:
Who could help/assist you with finding out about/getting your new timetable?

. . . .

After you have found out more about your new timetable:

How did finding out about your new timetable go?

. . . .

. . . .

. . . .

Did anything make you excited?

. . . .

. . . .

. . . .

Did anything make you worried?

. . . .

. . . .

. . . .

Are there any things you need to remember?

. . . .

. . . .

. . . .

Are there any things you would like help with?

. . . .

. . . .

. . . .

You may want to stick or draw your new timetable here

My new timetable:

Time	Monday	Tuesday	Wednesday	Thursday	Friday
08:00					
09:00					
10:00					
11:00					
12:00					
13:00					
14:00					
15:00					

What else is important to me?

The next section will help you think about anything else that is important to you when planning your transition to your new secondary school.

We have included some things that are important to other children when they transition to secondary school in the next few pages. Just fill in the pages that have things on them that are important to you. We have also left some space for you to add things that we might not have included.

Sensitive spots

Some children can find certain places in their new secondary school quite tricky – their 'sensitive spots'. For example, some children find crowded corridors or the canteen might seem too loud and busy. The toilets might also be a 'sensitive spot' because they might be a bit messy, or just very different to the toilets at home.

'SAFE HAVENS'

It is important to some people to find out where some 'safe havens' might be. These 'safe havens' could be quiet spaces you can go if things are getting too much, you need some time alone, or you want to talk to someone by yourself. Some schools will have special rooms that you can go to for a bit of 'time out'.

Is that something that could be important for you?

☐ I would like to think about my 'sensitive spots' in advance i.e. before I start my new secondary school [tick the box if you agree].

☐ I would like to know where my 'safe haven(s)' could be [tick the box if you agree].

☐ I would like to visit my 'safe haven(s)' at my new secondary school [tick if you agree].

If you ticked any of the box(es) above:
Who could help/assist you with thinking about your 'sensitive spots' and where your 'safe haven(s)' could be?

. . . .

After you have found out more about your 'sensitive spots' and 'safe havens':

How did finding out about your 'sensitive spots' and 'safe havens' go?

. . . .

. . . .

Did anything make you excited?

. . . .

. . . .

Did anything make you worried?

. . . .

. . . .

Are there any things you need to remember?

. . . .

. . . .

Are there any things you would like help with?

. . . .

. . . .

What would I like to share about myself?

Some young people find it helpful to share that they have an autism spectrum disorder (ASD) so that they can get support and help for their needs.

Some children may only share their diagnosis (that they have an ASD) with one other person in private, away from everyone else. Other people might want to tell everyone including their teachers, friends and other people they will meet at their new secondary school.

It isimportant to think about what is the most helpful thing to do with someone you know well, like your parents and/or your primary school teacher(s).

☐ I would like to think about whether it would be helpful to me to share that I have a diagnosis of an autism spectrum disorder with people at my new secondary school [tick the box if you agree].

☐ I would like to speak to my parents about sharing my diagnosis of ASD [tick the box if you agree].

☐ I would like to speak to my primary school teacher(s) about sharing my diagnosis of ASD [tick the box if you agree].

If you ticked any of the box(es) above:
Who could help/assist you with thinking about sharing that you have a diagnosis of ASD?

. . . .

After you have thought about sharing your diagnosis of ASD:

How did thinking about sharing your diagnosis of ASD go?

. . . .

. . . .

Did anything make you excited?

. . . .

. . . .

Did anything make you worried?

. . . .

. . . .

Are there any things you need to remember?

. . . .

. . . .

. . . .

Are there any things you would like help with?

. . . .

. . . .

. . . .

. . . .

Managing my first day

My first day at secondary school

For lots of children the first day of secondary school is very exciting but can also make them quite nervous. Getting started can feel difficult.

On the first day, some children find it helpful to get to the new secondary school *earlier* than the other children. Some children find it helpful to get to the new secondary school *later*, after all the other children have arrived. And some children find it helpful to *meet someone that they have met before* like a child who was in their primary school too, or a teacher they have met on a previous visit to the new secondary school.

It might be important to you to think about what would be most helpful on your first day of secondary school. It might be a good idea to talk to your parents, your primary school teacher(s) and/or your new secondary school teacher(s) and ask what they think might be helpful?

☐ I would like to think about whether it would be helpful to me to go into school earlier, later or meet someone I have met before on my first day at my new secondary school [tick the box if you agree].

☐ I would like to speak to my parents about managing my first day of secondary school [tick the box if you agree].

☐ I would like to speak to my primary school teacher(s) about managing my first day of secondary school [tick the box if you agree].

☐ I would like to speak to my secondary school teacher(s) about managing my first day of secondary school [tick the box if you agree].

If you ticked any of the box(es) above:
Who could help/assist you with thinking about your first day at your new secondary school?

. . . .

After you have thought about your first day of secondary school:

How did thinking about your first day of secondary school go?

. . . .

. . . .

Did anything make you excited?

. . . .

. . . .

Did anything make you worried?

. . . .

. . . .

Are there any things you need to remember?

. . . .

. . . .

. . . .

Are there any things you would like help with?

. . . .

. . . .

. . . .

Making friends

For some children meeting new people and making friends can be quite exciting, but for other children this might be quite scary.

It might be useful to think about how *you* feel about meeting new people by using the worry thermometer below. Draw an arrow to show where you are on the worry thermometer.

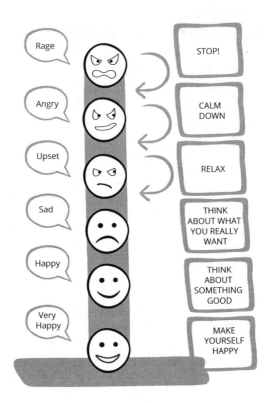

It might be important to you to have the opportunity to meet someone from your primary school who is also going to your secondary school. It might also be important to you, when you start secondary school, to meet other children with similar interests to you.

☐ I would like to meet someone from my primary school who is also going to my new secondary school [tick the box if you agree].

☐ I would like to meet other children at my new secondary school who have similar interests to me [tick the box if you agree].

If you ticked either of the box(es) above:
Who could help/assist you with thinking about meeting new people and making friends at your new secondary school?

. . . .

After you have thought about meeting new people and making friends at your new secondary school:

How did thinking about meeting new people and making friends at your new secondary school go?

. . . .

. . . .

Did anything make you excited?

. . . .

. . . .

Did anything make you worried?

. . . .

. . . .

Are there any things you need to remember?

. . . .

. . . .

. . . .

Are there any things you would like help with?

. . . .

. . . .

. . . .

Bullying

Bullying is when one person, or a group of people, intentionally behaves in a way that upsets another person. Sometimes this might be *saying* things that are not very nice, or it might be *physically* hurting someone, like hitting or kicking them.

Bullying is *always* wrong and should *never* be allowed.

It might be important to you to find out what the school rules are about bullying, what to do if you think you are being bullied, and who to see or talk to about it.

☐ I would like to find out what the school rules are about bullying at my new secondary school [tick the box if you agree].

☐ I would like to think about what to do and who to talk to if I think I am being bullied [tick the box if you agree].

If you ticked either of the box(es) above:

Who could help/assist you with finding out about the school rules on bullying, and what to do or who to see if you think you are being bullied at your new secondary school?

. . . .

After you have found out about the school rules on bullying, and what to do or who to see if you think you are being bullied at your new secondary school:

How did finding out about the school rules on bullying, and what to do or who to see if you think you are being bullied, go?

. . . .

. . . .

Did anything make you excited?

. . . .

. . . .

Did anything make you worried?

. . . .

. . . .

Are there any things you need to remember?

. . . .

. . . .

. . . .

Are there any things you would like help with?

. . . .

. . . .

. . . .

Homework:

Homework is a task children need to do at home. The aim of the homework is to help children fully understand what they have been taught in each lesson.

Some children are excited about getting more homework when they go to their new secondary school. Other children find more homework hard to manage.

At lots of secondary schools, children are given a 'planner' or 'homework diary' to help them organise what homework they have to do, and when they have to finish it by.

It might be important to you to find out what the school rules are about homework. It might also be helpful for you to ask someone from your new secondary school some questions about homework like the examples below:

- How will I know what my homework is?

- How will I know when the homework needs to be finished and handed in?

- How much time should I spend on homework each night?

☐ I would like to find out what the school rules are about homework at my new secondary school [tick the box if you agree].

☐ I would like to ask someone at my new secondary school about homework [tick the box if you agree].

If you ticked either of the box(es) above:
Who could help/assist you with finding out about the school rules on homework, and who to talk to about homework at your new secondary school?

. . . .

After you have found out about the school rules on homework, and who to talk to about homework at your new secondary school:

How did finding out about the school rules on homework, and who to talk to about homework at your new secondary school, go?

. . . .

. . . .

Did anything make you excited?

. . . .

. . . .

Did anything make you worried?

. . . .

. . . .

Are there any things you need to remember?

. . . .

. . . .

. . . .

Are there any things you would like help with?

. . . .

. . . .

. . . .

Is there anything else that is important to me?

We have left you some space here to think about anything else that might be important to you when planning your transition to secondary school.

Some final bits and bobs

Things I want to happen when I go to my new secondary school...

It might be useful for you to think about the main things that you want to happen when you go to your new secondary school. It might be useful to look back over the pages of this workbook and see which boxes you ticked.

You can use this workbook to show others the things that are important to you. You can also take this workbook to any meetings you have about your new secondary school.

And finally: things I will need...

In primary school your teacher(s) usually gave you everything you needed for different lessons. At your new secondary school, you will need to bring your own equipment for each lesson.

It might be useful for you to use the equipment checklist on the following page to tick off things you need to buy, or take with you to secondary school.

☐ I would like to find out about what equipment I will need at my new secondary school [tick the box if you agree].

If you ticked the box above:

Who could help/assist you with finding out about what equipment you will need at your new secondary school?

. . . .

Equipment checklist

- ☐ Pencils
- ☐ Pens
- ☐ Rubber/eraser
- ☐ Colouring pens/pencils
- ☐ Ruler
- ☐ Pencil sharpener
- ☐ Scissors
- ☐ Calculator
- ☐ Pencil case
- ☐ Notebooks/paper
- ☐ Folders
- ☐ Lunchbox/money for lunch
- ☐ House keys
- ☐ New school uniform
- ☐ New PE kit
- ☐ New school bag
- ☐ ....
- ☐ ....
- ☐ ....
- ☐ ....

We hope that this Transition Workbook has been helpful and that you feel ready to go to your new secondary school.

Good luck with your transition!

Please *do not* write in
this workbook. To use book
for skills practice, you
may photocopy sheets.